Boise

The City and The People

TEXT BY CLAY MORGAN

PHOTOGRAPHY BY STEVE BLY

To the old gang.
C.M.

To Pam, who has given me
my dreams, and to everyone who
encouraged me to pursue
this new career.
S.B.

Above: Salmon River
whitewater: rafting the
"bounding main."
Top: Pete Skamzer trout
fishing on the Boise River.

Title page: Idaho's capitol.
Back cover, top: On The Grove.
Bottom: Carriage rides are a
year-round delight in
downtown Boise.

Library of Congress
Cataloging-in-Publication Data
Morgan, Clay.
    Boise : the city and the people / text by
Clay Morgan ; photography by Steve Bly.
        p.   cm.
    Includes index.
    ISBN 1-56037-045-9
    1. Boise (Idaho)--Geography. I. Title.
F754.B65M67 1993   93-27515
979.6'28--dc20

Text © 1993 Clay Morgan
Photography © 1993 Steve Bly
© 1993 American & World Geographic
Publishing. All rights reserved.

All design, editorial, and typesetting completed
in the USA. Printed in Korea by Sung In Print-
ing, Inc. of San Mateo, CA.

Contents

Above: Winter snows often push mule deer into Boise.
Top: The "vertical environment" of the Bruneau
River canyon.

The Sense of the City

A Center at the Edge

To get a sense of this city, stand at its center. Stand on Boise's Capitol Boulevard bridge and look over the state capitol's dome to the mountains. There begin the vast boreal forests expanding north through Canada. North lies a land of blue and green and, for much of the year, white.

Now, turn and look south past the Spanish tower of the Morrison-Knudsen railway depot. South stretch the great Western deserts, widening their palette of tans and reds all the way into Mexico.

Boise marks a geographic center of continental significance, a joining of two enormous bio-regions: the wetter-and-cooler North and the hotter-and-drier South. Both are natural wonderlands mainly empty of humans. As cities go, Boise is still a babe in a wilderness, and with luck it will be all the better for it.

Boise also straddles an historical dividing line. On one side is the Great Northwest of Scotch-English and French influence. On the other side is the Great Southwest of Spanish and Mexican pedigree. From the Boise area north, many place names and geographical labels read French: *Boise, Bruneau, Coeur d'Alene* and *Pend Oreille; coulee, butte, prairie* and *crevasse.*

Not far to the south, the accent changes. State names read Spanish: *Nevada, California, Arizona, New Mexico.* Our word "cowboy" remembers *caballero*; "buckaroo" recalls *vaquero*; and our old western term for jail, "hoosegow," derives from the Spanish *juzgado.*

Of course, history didn't start with French and Spanish. Native Americans were first to use the Boise area. Their stories are written on the many pictographs found in the desert, and many of their words survive as Idaho place names: *Nampa, Lochsa, Benewah* and *Shoshone.*

And history never stops. It certainly isn't stopping now for Boise. Presently, Boise straddles a line between the over-peopled California and the quickly populating Northern Rocky Mountains.

That's North and South. There are also Up and Down. Look upriver and know that this clean water has come down from the snows of the lofty Sawtooth Mountains, as close and wild as winter's promise. Look downstream and consider that this same water will boil down through Hells Canyon, the deepest

The Boise River's headwaters: Sawtooth Mountains lakes.

Owyhee River country.

gorge in North America and a devil's cauldron in summer.

Keep watching the river. It's moving. It's clean. It is home to fox, deer, mink and raccoon, and to heron, kingfisher, mallard and eagle. Its riverside cottonwoods are harvested by beaver. In summer, you'll see it filled with humans, beating the heat and enjoying each other. At any season, you'll see men and women fishing, casting their lines for rainbow and steelhead. Behind these fisherfolk, in every weather, you'll see the great-spirited Greenbelters, enjoying the city-long riverside park, walking, jogging, blading and biking.

The Boise River is the pride of Boise. It is the symbol of Boise and its reason for being. But stand on this bridge for very long and you'll notice the rumble of the auto traffic. That river may be in motion, but so is the city.

This much is plain to an outsider. Boise is something other than just *busy*. It is not a hurrying town. Boiseans are where they want to be, already. The city is not "laid back," although it's relaxed.

Right: Lunker trout on patrol at the Morrison-Knudsen Nature Center. **Below:** Nearby, a fisherman tries Park Center Pond.

The finely restored Morrison-Knudsen Depot.

And "boom town" is too easy a term to describe it. If one were pressed to portray Boise's present condition one might call it a flowering. Granted, it is a flowering of unlikely hybrids. A corporate exec in a kayak is business as usual. A fly fisherman in a wheelchair is normal.

Boise is a small, blooming city in a mighty big place, at the center of a wild world. Boise has the sense of both a center and an edge. This is not a contradiction; it is a tremendous strength. Sociologically, Boise is an urban oasis on the edge of vast and empty public lands. Economically, Boise's present feels solid and its future looks bright. The center holds. The edge supports. For now.

Perhaps socially and economically Boise has a sort of evolutionary edge. We humans thrive when we can live on edges. Through the ages, we succeeded best when we explored our world's edges. First we pushed out of the forest onto the savanna and opened up our horizons. Then we went down to the seashore and built our ships and we pushed back our horizons. We're going into space now; perhaps the ruddy escarpment of a mountain range on Mars will be our next "edge" to live on. Going to that edge—and looking over it—will be as human as falling off a log.

Most of us express this affinity for edges when we choose a place to live. Whenever we look for the ideal home, we look for the river run, for the mountain view, for the opening in the cottonwoods where deer sometimes cross at dawn and dusk (those temporal edges of night and day). Give us a view, we say.

Give us a place with an edge, a place that catches change—any change—from mountain to prairie, from city to farmland, from pioneer to modern, from lull to storm.

It works with geography, landscape, architecture, history, weather and seasons. It works with cities and homes. It works in Boise. The expansive Foothills home with the spectacular view has this exciting, livable edge-ness, and so does the genteel East End

Hyde Park

bungalow tucked beneath a wall of rimrock.

Life on edges like Boise's cuts through daily routines and protects against dullness of mind and spirit. It gives lives a sense of pioneering a daily frontier. Many people live in Boise precisely to cultivate that sense, to hone their own edges and to sharpen their enjoyment of life. They live in Boise because Boise is on the edge.

Boise is also a center. It is a center of commerce, government, transportation, education and culture. And of controversy. It is a gathering of people in the sparsely populated American West. It is the urban "Up Front" to the great Idaho "Out Back." It is a cultural "here" in the great "out there."

For the most part, Boiseans count themselves lucky to live here during times which at best might be called "interesting" in the rest of the world. Boise, at this moment, has all the right elements: strong economy, tight community, ethnic tolerance, clean environment, safe streets, good schools, great parks, budding arts, nearby wilderness and immense public lands, and the positive attention of the rest of the country.

Of course all the right elements have the ingredients to go wrong. A strong center attracts like a magnet attracts—by the principle of opposites—both good and bad. Will boom town overbuild? Will schools overcrowd? Will crime force itself into the creases caused by community growth? Will protecting the environment in the face of so many newcomers result in making Nature "Off Limits" to all?

Whatever happens, Boise will remain both a center and an edge. As a center of good will and cooperative spirits, remedies for social ills will work better here than elsewhere. As an urban edge set inside a vast natural treasure, environmental safeguards have a chance to succeed. Center and edge. Body and soul. At this point in its history, Boise has it both ways.

Left: Cedar waxwing, a Boise winter resident.
Below: Guaranteed peacefulness in Kathryn Albertson Park.

The Singular City

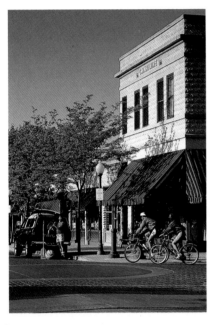

Hyde Park is a hangout for outdoor enthusiasts.

Facing page, top: *"Alive After Five," after work, downtown.* **Bottom:** *Main Street, with the Tour Train on its trail of tales.*

Boise might be the exception that proves a rule—the rule that says that in modern America, cities have to be anxious, hassly, and dangerous. Calluses, creativity and care combine to keep Boise cheerful and livable.

Boise works. Right now, it is working well. It works hard, plays hard, and dreams big dreams, while it maintains a livability higher than similar cities—especially those that do not have nearby megalopolises to attract away crime and grime.

Boise has no slums. It has lower income neighborhoods, certainly, but most stay well kept and many maintain a healthful, rural character. One telling statistic about Boise's poor is that Idaho is among the top four states, nationally, in the percentage of people who work two or more jobs. Of course, they work two jobs because they *have* to, but a strong work ethic keeps many Boiseans off welfare. It is also one reason high-tech companies like to locate in Boise.

Another reason is the low rate of crime. Recently, Boise attracted national wonderment for going more than a year without a murder. That was due to good luck, of course. Crime exists in Boise, and it increases with the city's population. But in 1990, Boise's major crime rate was 558 per 10,000 citizens, compared to over 800 for Spokane, Reno and Salem, and over 1,250 for Salt Lake City. Much of the larceny that happens in Boise, happens because good folks don't lock up. They're not accustomed to—and frankly, they don't want to. They rely on luck, and on their neighbors keeping an eye out.

Boise has developed a full complement of business necessities: convenient transportation, modern communications, a motivated work force, and a workable infrastructure for corporate support. It has gathered together the municipal wherewithal: good police and fire protection; two large, rapidly expanding hospitals; a good public school system; and a growing urban university.

The city has cultivated its cultural amenities: the best night life within a long day's drive; great restaurants; a ballet; opera; symphony; Shakespeare; art galleries; a premier performing arts facility; perhaps too many cinemas; and more softball teams and coffeehouses than

"Suspense with the bottom dropping out": South Fork of the Payette.

any other former cowtown around.

Boise has the good luck of a geographic location that offers four-season beauty. Its three-ecosystem personality—high desert, mountain forest, riverine woods—supports outdoor sports for almost every inclination. One sport has distinguished the city, of late. Although Boise has the healthful, semiarid climate that most people think it has, it is also a whitewater capital

to the world. Boise is where rafters and *'yakers* come from all over, in order to get ready to really get wet.

Boise has engaged the popular support of its citizens. Volunteerism in Boise is nothing short of phenomenal. And individual and corporate generosity—in the form of gifts, bequests, and public-private-corporate partnerships—has molded the beauty and the character of the city.

This participation of the

people in the life of a city has been seen as essential to civilization since ancient Greece. Boiseans seem to understand that if they're not helping out, they're standing in the way. In Boise, few citizens stand in the way. In 1907, Clarence Darrow called Boise "the Athens of the sagebrush." In 1976, when Idaho's U.S. Senator Frank Church declared his candidacy for the presidency, *Washington Post* columnist David Broder was so taken by the energy of the city that he asked his wife to fly out from Washington to share the experience. More recently, at the Morrison Center, singer Joan Baez stopped her performance to call Boise "the intimate metropolis."

Boise may be intimate, but it is not reserved. In 1993, 46 citizens filed applications for an open seat on the City Council. These candidates, by and large, were not seeking office to make great changes. They wanted to help in directing the current surge of the city. Democracy in Boise is direct and demanding. Hardly a development gets done without first demonstrating its worth.

These days, Boise is booming, blooming, and beaming. Although Boiseans know this, sometimes outsiders need charts and comparisons. But comparisons are difficult when you are the only one. And because Boise is the only real city in sight, to people from L.A. and New York, Boise can seem almost village-like. It can seem bucolic—even sleepy—and so *downright safe* that to people from places of greater paranoia, it can almost be unnerving. People in Boise can come across so friendly and concerned, that sometimes it's like you're in one of those sci-fi movies where *something has happened but you're not sure what*. A reporter for *USA Today* once came to Boise and asked, "What is everybody smiling for?" Everybody had a different answer.

Such reactions to Boise are usually limited to those who "fly through." To those who come to live, Boise can seem a dream come true. These people are the ones smiling the most. According to urban historian Todd Shallat, Boise shines as "the city of their own lost youths," for many of the people moving—or wanting to move—to Boise. Mike Weber, a native Boisean who works at Hewlett-Packard, said that many California emigrants at HP are "happy as heck" to

have transferred to Boise. Many feel they have escaped.

So much for the views of outsiders newly arrived. To folks from the surrounding hamlets of Bliss, Vale, Cascade and Garden Valley, Boise can seem to offer too much: excitement and aggravation; sophistication and superiority; nonstop shopping and one-way streets; and almost incredible 15-minute traffic jams that suddenly fade to streets of desertion. Admitting governmental and commercial dependence, people from the *other* Idaho have sometimes called Boise, the "Center of the Universe." They say this, half in jest and half in admiration. And, one might add, half in relief. One big city is "plenty enough" in a state whose people treasure open spaces.

Boise is it, the only Big Show. According to the U.S. Census, Boise is the only Metropolitan Statistical Area (MSA) in Idaho, which is presently the most rural state in the nation. Only one Idaho county—Boise's Ada—has more than 50,000 residents. Every other state, including Alaska, has a more urbanized population, meaning that a greater percentage of its residents live in heavily populat-

ed areas. Boise's MSA population now stands at a quarter-million. A recent estimate puts the in-city population at 135,000.

In a big land with few people, Boise stands out. Not only is Boise Idaho's capital, it is also the only urban center for miles around. Spokane and Salt Lake City, Boise's nearest big neighbors, lie 300 air miles to the north and southeast. Boise's other two big neighbors, Portland and Seattle, lie farther: 350 and 400 miles. When you draw a radius 300 miles around, encircling 90,000 square miles, you snare a lot of potential visitors and customers. Arbitron estimates Boise's market area of "dominant influence" to be over 400,000 people. That's out of one of America's emptiest quarters: southern Idaho, eastern Oregon, and northern Nevada.

This all accounts for two important qualities of Boise. The first quality is that, for its modest size, Boise offers a disproportionate number of urban qualities. As Idaho's capital and a busy center for federal agencies, Boise functions as the place where the legislature lays down the state's laws and Feds direct national programs. As the

California quail (left) and Canada geese (below) winter in Idaho.

Facing page: *Autumn delights along the Boise River.*

Glimpses of life in lively downtown.

chief trading post and watering hole between Salt Lake and Seattle, Boise serves as business center and cultural oasis to a great big area, encompassing the residents of three states and many people just passing through.

The second aspect that although Boise is isolated, it is by no means insular: Boiseans themselves *get out and go.* Boiseans share the western love of driving and of "seeing country." While weekends are usually spent among natural wonders near the city, vacations often venture far afield. Boise is served by major airlines, Amtrak, and Interstate 84, making it easy to get out of town, and get back. A Manhattanite has to leave his office some hours before a flight out of New York. At the Boise Air Terminal, you park near the front door. The Boise end of any trip to any other city is usually the easiest end of that trip.

Also, because Boise's population lately has been swelling with newcomers, Boiseans tend to be more cosmopolitan than geography might suggest. At least eight large corporations keep Boise as their headquarters, and others maintain some of their largest operations here. Boise's "tran-

sients" are often transient professionals, here for meetings with their corporate bosses.

For many newcomers, the first view of the city is from the Boise airport, or from the I-84 freeway exit at Broadway Avenue. Either way, Boise looks compact—and brimming with trees. This view—minus buildings—is similar to the view of Boise by the first Euro-Americans who visited here. Legend has it that in 1811 the Astorians barely survived crossing the dry Snake River Plains. When they saw the Boise valley they shouted, *"Les Bois! Les Bois!"* which translates, roughly, to *"(gasp!) (cough!) (wheeze!) Trees!"*

Later, more than 50,000 Oregon Trail travelers followed a route roughly parallel to the present day freeway, and doubtless they reveled at the sight of greenery. Their stock likely bolted at the scent of water, while they rumbled down over the lava rimrock and headed into the green valley.

The view from the heights above the Boise Canyon's outlet provides both relief and excitation. The dark summertime green makes the first impression. Boise now has

about a quarter-million trees, or one for every person. The city's peripheral colors are no less impressive. The pale yellow-purple of desert to the left and the dun-to-blue-green of the mountains to the right frame this scene with intertwining lines that seem to run right up to one's feet.

The historic Owyhee Mountains rise to the southwest. These were named after "O-wy-hee" (Hawaii) Islanders whom the Northwest Fur Trading Company brought here to trap beaver, in 1810, and who were never heard from again. South and west, and out of sight, but only 25 miles away, flows the mighty Snake River, through the half-million-acre National Birds of Prey Area, where North America's greatest and most varied population of raptors congregate every spring.

Beginning with the nearer, southern horizons, several natural terraces, which Boiseans call "the benches," stairstep down into the valley from their highest elevation, on Ten Mile Ridge. Neighborhoods and shopping centers now fill the lower two benches.

The heart of the city beats on the valley floor: old and new neighborhoods, corporate campuses, Boise State Uni-

Above: *"Paint the Town" volunteer day helps seniors spruce up homes.*
Top: *Neighborhoods in nature—River Run.*
Right: *Boise offers many high tech jobs—this one at Micron Technology.*

The Moore-Cunningham home on Warm Springs Avenue pioneered geothermal energy.

versity, and the city-long system of large parks and river trails, which has become the pride of Boise.

Important landmarks visible from many other outlooks over Boise include that Boise River Greenbelt, which seems to stretch toward the horizon; Table Rock Butte, whose quarried stone built the state capitol and other buildings; the Capitol itself and other large structures, including the 1930 art-deco Hoff Building; and the newer "classy-glassy" high-rises along Main Street and elsewhere.

The Spanish-mission–style Morrison-Knudsen Depot anchors the south end of Capitol Boulevard. Nearer the river, the most obvious structure is probably Bronco Stadium, with its brilliant white floodlights and royal blue artificial turf. A corporate headquarters village lies just upriver from the stadium, and far downriver, up on the first bench, spreads Hewlett-Packard's large design and fabrication center. Towne Square shopping mall dominates the southwest sector, and the Boise airport commands a high bench on the south side. Up on Shafer Butte, the highest point above Boise, Bogus Basin shines as a wintertime beacon, with its many acres of lighted night skiing.

The most dramatic entry to Boise is by way of the I-84 Connector, which takes one at freeway speeds right at the mountains. But the more esthetic way in is along beautiful Warm Springs Avenue, which begins at the golf course at the base of Table Rock and passes the grounds of the Old Penitentiary. Here many Idaho criminals spent their "periods of confinement," and many Boise children spent their idyllic childhoods on the hills just above the Pen, idly hunting arrowheads and watching the prisoners loiter below them in the yard. The Old Pen is now a remarkable historical museum and the grounds now a beautiful botanical garden. Castle Rock rises just west of the Pen. Castle Rock is a favorite of runners and scramblers, and Idaho's Indians say it is hallowed ground.

Warm Springs Avenue heads west toward downtown, past many of Boise's finest and oldest homes, one dating back to 1868. Many of these homes were financed by Boise Basin gold. Another earth treasure—geothermal water—still warms them today, thoroughly and economically, as it does the Capitol buildings and many homes in the city. Extensive geothermal development is part of Boise's singularity. Boise is the only major U.S. city blessed with reliable geothermal heat bubbling up beneath its feet.

On the left, behind the great homes, newer homes, great and small, are filling the area between the avenue and the riverside park land. This area boasts the best place to hang out in Boise: the Morrison-Knudsen Wildlife Interpretive Center, where wild geese nest and big trout "lunker up" in a naturalistic, minnow's-eye-view, Idaho-stream aquarium.

Idaho Street begins where Warms Springs Avenue ends. To the right, spreads a district sometimes called "the Near East End," which includes rapidly expanding St. Luke's Hospital, professionals' offices, and many handsome homes. Behind this area, and up against the foothills sits the old Fort Boise. The Fort Grounds include major city sports and cultural facilities, the Federal Building, the VA Hospital, and some of the loveliest and loneliest-looking places in Boise. Back in the shade against the hills hide the old brick-and-stone officers' quarters. Behind the hill, up in Mountain Cove, lie the Fort's historic cemetery and the final resting place of Civil War-era soldiers and early Boise citizens.

On the left of Idaho Street and fronted by Main Street, sits the almost cubical U.S. Assay Office, which once "proofed" Boise Basin gold. It was built with two-foot thick walls in 1872, for $77,000. Gold worth $75 million passed through its vaults by 1933. One of the first "monumental" buildings constructed in the region, the Assay Office now houses State offices.

"Old Boise"—the commercial and restaurant district around Sixth and Main streets west of the Assay Office—dates to the century's first decade. "Old Boise" jumps lively at night, especially on those long and musical, spring and summer evenings. Noodles Italian Restaurant, Tom Grain's saloon, and the Moxie Java espresso house are three of the city's favorite pubs.

Culinary culture is important to the city. Boise has always been an important travelers' rest. In the 1840s, Fort Boise stood as almost the only established supply station along the entire Oregon Trail.

Today, Boise remains the stopover-of-choice on the long road between Salt Lake and Seattle. Historically, geography explained the situation. But in the last twenty years, Boise has come into its own as city of fine restaurants and public houses. Pug Ostling, owner of Noodles, compared Boise to Spokane. He claimed, "Boise has half the population, but twice the fizz." Why? To a degree, Ostling credited Boise's large corporate community. "The execs know what restaurants should be like."

Of course, the life and times of the restaurateur are fraught with peril, in Boise just as in New York. Ostling said that in the early 1970s, the Sandpiper restaurant "owned" the Boise dining scene, as a California-style steak house. Then, the large chains moved in and sliced up the pie. More recently, a second wave of chain restaurants has arrived, including General Foods' Red Lobster and The Olive Garden. National chains pose local restaurants a formidable challenge, because of their financial resources, polished advertising, and the efficiencies and economics of scale.

But local restaurateurs respond with individual charm,

specialty dishes, and personal service. Boise may have many chain restaurants offering good products, but the "independents" of Boise are remarkable. A short list would include Ostling's Noodles, as well as Amore, Angell's, The Beanery, The Gamekeeper, Louie's, Peter Schott's, and The Renaissance. Boise continues to attract more restaurants. In 1991, the city issued 31 new licenses.

Southwest of Old Boise is the old—and new—Basque

One big city is "plenty enough" in a state whose people treasure open spaces.

Row. Boise lays claim to a cultural singularity: the largest Basque community outside of Europe. The Basque Center, the Basque Museum, and Bar Gernika form the physical center of this community, and the Basque spirit is infused throughout Boise.

Idaho Street hits city center at Capitol Boulevard, with the state capitol to the right, City Hall to the left, and the MK Depot across the river to the

Above: *Pharaoh's gargoyle on the Egyptian Theater.*
Top: *The Old Penitentiary is now a fascinating museum.*
Right: *Boise's grande dame, the Idanha Hotel.*

Above: *The Idaho Botanical Gardens, beside the Old Pen.*
Top: *Beaux Arts Christmas Sale at the Boise Art Museum.*

left, past the university and parks. The Boise Centre-on-the-Grove convention center, the 8th Street Marketplace, and the downtown core form the vital heart of the city.

The Roman Revival state capitol is modeled after the nation's capitol in Washington, D.C. Construction began in 1905 and finished in 1920, at a cost of $2 million. Built of Table Rock sandstone, the capitol houses some beautiful art. The most recent additions are the magnificent woven murals by Dana Boussard, depicting the histories and geographies of Idaho's three regions.

Boise's handsomest building is perhaps the Idanha Hotel. Done in French chateau style, with three round turrets, it was the most expensive building in the city—at $125,000—when it was completed 1901.

The 11-story Hoff Building was originally the Hotel Boise, built in 1930 in an art deco style, which will always be artistically suspect. It still has its beautiful marble interior, and its summit has been improved with a square copper turret. The Egyptian Theater is another Boise favorite. With its Spanish outside and its mock-Pharaonic interior,

the Egyptian has delighted Boiseans since it opened, just before talkies, in 1927.

Downtown Boise seems to be a "case in point" whenever people talk about American cities. It simultaneously attracts both promise and peril, and it has barely survived both misdirected good intentions and neglect. In 1973, former Boisean L.J. Davis wrote a now-famous *Harper's Magazine* article, "Tearing Down Boise," which chronicled the nearing death of the city's core. Davis wrote, "If things go on as they are, Boise stands an excellent chance of becoming the first American city to have deliberately eradicated itself...Boise is a dying city."

In a fit of "urban renewal," the city had undertaken the complete leveling of downtown, south of Main Street. Davis wrote, "Downtown Boise gives the impression that it has recently been visited by an exceedingly tidy bombing raid conducted by planes that cleaned up after themselves."

That was Phase I. Phase II would have torn down several blocks north of Main, making way for a suburban-style, enclosed shopping mall, which would have looked like every other American mall and

would have been ringed by parking lots. Fortunately, an "anchor" tenant was never found, and the slash-and-burn method of urban renewal was finally allowed to die.

But this didn't happen before many people were hurt. It tore out their hearts to see the city's heart torn down. In his 1980 book, *American Dreams: Lost & Found*, Studs Terkel quoted a Boise singer and songwriter of beautiful voice and vision. Regarding Boise in the 1970s, Rosalie Sorrells said, "Boise hardly exists for me anymore. All the things I remember with pleasure have been torn down. It used to be like a little cup of trees. A river runs right through the middle. You could hardly see more than two or three buildings. The statehouse and Hotel Boise. Just trees and this river. Oh, corridors of green."

And Sorrells wasn't being a country-girl provincial. She said she loved cities and she loved New York. But it seems Boise had broken her heart.

Now Boise is Big Time. A real city skyline has risen high above the trees. And fortunately, a lot more has risen since the Big Sink of the '70s, including investments in parks and places for people. Another Boise artist, Peter Johnson, said in 1993, "For years, Boise was ruins, ruins, ruins. Now, it's a beautiful thing."

It had taken until then for downtown Boise to get ready to thrive again. Several handsome corporate buildings had been built. There was a new city hall, and for most of its downtown section, Main Street looked great. On harder-hit Idaho Street, The Bon Marche was expanding its offerings, and the Mode building was to see refurbishment, as will the Simplot Building. U.S. Bank planned to construct an 11-story Idaho headquarters. Its "Capital Plaza" might be a most important addition, a mixed-use commercial and *residential* tower intended to bring people back actually to live downtown.

A thriving convention center has been built on a new and attractive public square called "The Grove." The Boise Centre has 87,000 square feet and a total capacity of 4,200 people. Its Marriott Food Service can serve 2,000 simultaneous meals. The Grove was also planned to be the site of a large hotel. As of late spring 1993, three groups of developers were vying for contract to build one.

Immediately south of The Grove, cars speed by the Boise Centre on the long-awaited Broadway-Chinden Connector. Some Boiseans fear that the throughway will turn out to be more of a Boise "divider." But early indications were that it would indeed better connect downtown with the city's population center, to the west.

The renovation south of Main Street has all but obliterated an important part of Boise's history. Chinese families once called this section home. For a time after the mining days, Boise had the largest Chinese population in the Northwest. And for decades they grew and sold vegetables in the city. The Chinese were proud, industrious and valuable Boise citizens. They were often discriminated against, but they created a vibrant community. Part of their legacy is the undying, unfounded legend of extensive Chinese "tunnels," dug from basement to basement throughout Boise's downtown. This legend has sponsored countless "expeditions" by several generations of Boise children, through buildings and alleyways, in search of the past.

But not all of the past has been lost south of Main

Street. South of the Connector lies an old warehouse district that harbors the charming 8th Street Marketplace, the Esther Simplot Academy for the Performing Arts, the city library, the Table Rock brew pub, and The Flicks movie theater.

To the north of downtown

Downtown Boise seems to be a "case in point" whenever people talk about American cities.

lies the fabled North End, whose tree shaded neighborhoods provide endless architectural variety. Beyond downtown, and ever westward, greater Boise spreads, including the Towne Square shopping mall and the Memorial Stadium baseball park, home of Boise's pride, the Hawks.

Boise's Foothills neighborhoods rise conspicuously against the mountains. They begin with Warm Springs Mesa in Boise's far east and then march, hill by hill, west by northwest, clear to the town of Eagle. The views from these homes are absolutely stirring.

Special Events

In May 1993 when Steve Schmader announced that the upcoming Boise River Festival would include a visit by Walt Disney's gigantic Magic Kingdom balloon, he said, "Imagine something the size of the West One Bank building floating overhead." But Disney's balloon was only a small part of this Boise event that grew in three years from an interesting concept to an enormous success.

River Giants Parade at the Boise River Festival.

Events characterize cities much as skylines and food specialties do. Portland's Rose Festival and Spokane's Bloomsday celebrate nature and renewal. In Boise, the main event is the Boise River Festival, and this late June festivity celebrates Boise for what it is: a family town that loves where it is—on the banks of a beautiful river.

With some 400 sponsors and 3,000 volunteers, the Festival has included "SkyFire" spectacular fireworks displays; a "Nite Lite" parade of lighted floats down the river; a "River Giants" parade of inflatable characters down Capitol Boulevard; hot air balloon rallies; a Blue Angels air show; music and entertain-

The fireworks finale.

ment; and over two dozen sports competitions.

The Festival premiered in 1991 to an aggregate attendance of 310,000. Two years later the attendance had nearly doubled. The Festival's popularity is everything organizers hoped for, but it prompted some rethinking. For one thing, the river floats parade was reassigned to Capital Boulevard so crowds won't hurt the river's fragile banks. Schmader hopes for something similar to Disneyland's Electric Parade.

The River Festival isn't the only peculiar-to-Boise event. A wild midsummer's midnight relay footrace runs through the Sawtooth Mountains from Stanley to Boise. The Idaho International

Women's Challenge has established itself as the world's premier Pro-Am women's bicycle race, covering hundreds of miles over many days, with thousands of feet of elevation gains. And a springtime Race to Robie Creek encourages 2,000 runners to hump the old toll road from Fort Boise over the Boise Mountains, on a 13-mile half-crazy, half marathon, which has to be the toughest race loved by so many people.

All these activities ought to wear Boiseans out, but they can take their rests at other activities. "Alive After Five" on The Grove—Wednesday evenings in summer—is where Boiseans like to meet to plan how to exhaust themselves on weekends. And Boi-se State University provides them with opportunities to watch the best athletes exhaust *them*selves. BSU sports are hugely popular. The NCAA national outdoor track championships, an NCAA regional basketball tournament, and the Big Sky Conference basketball tournament all can be enjoyed at BSU's stadium and pavilion.

Other special events in Boise include the Great Potato Marathon, the Capitol Classic kids' footrace from the capitol to the depot; a "Paint the Town" volunteer day when Boiseans help the elderly by painting their homes; and a full-galleried Ben Hogan golf tournament.

But this list is not exhaustive.

Above: The "Magic Kingdom" soars above the Festival.
Below: As fleeting as childhood, a Festival sandcastle.

The Presence of the Past

The story of Boise's past is told everywhere. From the dramatic geological testament of Table Rock to the varied and harmonious Harrison Boulevard homes, the history of Boise is one great story.

If history is defined as the chronicle of change, then a lot of Boise history is being made right now. Each new immigrant changes the city. She contributes her personality to a vibrant mix. And she adds her pressures on city services to those of the many other newcomers.

Ada County is expected to grow by one third in the 1990s. As Boise urbanizes and becomes more cosmopolitan, it faces new challenges. Among those are the threats to its three-dimensional chronicles—those buildings, neighborhoods, mountains and bluffs that remind Boiseans of what life was like, back when.

Fortunately, Boise retains enough vestiges of its youth to delight both newcomers and old-timers. Although the city is not an antiquarian relic relying on old charms and the kindness of tourists, Boiseans do get to live near, next to, and often inside fine specimens of Boise's past.

The story of Boise's past is told everywhere. From the dramatic geological testament of Table Rock to the varied and harmonious Harrison Boulevard homes, the history of Boise is one great story.

Geology tells its part of that story through the mute representations of stone. The Boise area's geological past is, by turn, obvious, mysterious, and tantalizing. It is thought to include hot flows of lava, a giant lake, and scouring floods of Biblical proportions. Some geologists even suggest there was a nearby impact of an enormous meteor, although evidence for such an event is slim.

A geological story has to be translated to be told, and Boise has an able interpreter in Spencer Wood, geoscientist at Boise State University. As Dr. Wood describes it, Boise geology is dramatic. The scene one sees from almost any Boise doorstep is like a snapshot of the earth caught in the act of changing.

The most obvious geological feature is the Boise Mountains, climbing right out of town. They are part of the Idaho batholith, a massive chunk of granite, which rose out of the earth's crust some 80 million years ago because it was lighter than surrounding materials. Dig deep enough below the city, and you'll strike the granite again. And the Owyhee Mountains south of Boise are thought to be part of the same batholith. Cottonwood Creek canyon, just north of town, offers a good view of exposed Idaho granite.

Boise itself is built on thick deposits left by giant Lake Idaho, which existed from 8 million to 2.5 million years before the present. Lake Idaho disappeared when the Snake River's precursor river eroded its way through the heavy basalt near Weiser and opened a channel for drainage.

With Lake Idaho gone, the young Boise River began meandering its way back and forth across the lake gravels. Boise's several terraces, or "benches," were created by the river as it gouged out new banks. Each bench marks a former river flood plain. The First Bench was the last to be formed, more than 100,000 years ago.

Ancient lakes and rivers explain only a part of the area's past. Volcanoes and lava flows also added character. The rhyolites of Castle Rock are 14 million years old. The first basalt eruptions began about 1 million years ago, south of the city. More eruptions occurred at Smith Prairie, and flowed down the Boise River Canyon. Still other flows originated beyond Columbia Village. These lavas' temperatures would have

measured about 1100°C. The heavy basalts ran like water, at up to 20 and 30 miles per hour. The lighter rhyolites flowed more slowly, or else exploded.

Much of the volcanic activity occurred during humankind's time on earth, although before the paleo-Americans got to the Boise Valley. The Kuna Butte shield volcano, for example, is 300,000 years old. However, Boise's early residents were not unaware of the earth's inner power. About 7,000 years ago, Mt. Mazama erupted in Oregon, creating the structure for Crater Lake and blanketing Boise in several inches of ash. More recent eruptions at Craters of the Moon happened about 2,100 years ago. Spencer Wood says that early Boiseans "certainly sat here and watched the glow in the sky."

They may have watched from Table Rock, Boise's most identifiable geologic structure. Nowadays the goal of runners and mountain bikers, the nighttime retreat for Boise lovers, and the site of a large Christian cross, Table Rock owes its existence to Boise's most notable geologic feature: hot water.

Geothermal waters formed Table Rock by depositing lay-

er upon layer of fine sand to create the valuable, polishable sandstone used for the state capitol and many other buildings. Hot springs also served to transport and concentrate the Boise Basin gold that later made young Boise rich. During the gold rush era, over 2.3 million ounces of placer gold came out through Boise, and helped to develop the opulent Warm Springs Avenue.

More importantly perhaps, geothermal water gave Boise one of its claims to fame. Boise was the first city in the world to develop its geothermal resources as a major way of heating homes.

The restored 1892 pump house at Quarry View Park, by the Old Pen, offers a good place to study Boise's geological legacy. The exposed rhyolite outcrop known as Castle Rock is an upthrust portion of the 850-foot-deep rhyolite under the park, which serves as the aquifer for 172°F hot water. The quarries and rockpiles up on the hillside give mute testimony to the hard labor by prisoners who quarried stone for their own lock-up and many other Boise buildings. A climb up Castle Rock affords a vista of the Warm Springs residential district,

Artist Fred Choate's mural of Old Boise adorns the Pioneer Tent Building at 6th and Main.

Left: A Nez Perce child performs a traditional dance at the All Idaho Pow Wow.
Below: Fly-fishing heaven—Silver Creek Nature Conservatory.

whose homes are warmed by the natural hot water.

Rain and snowmelt in the Boise Mountains percolates down through cracks in the Idaho batholith to a depth of about a mile. The earth's heat warms the water and it rises by convection back toward the valley floor. Carbon-14 dating indicates that a drop of rainwater may take from 6,700 to 17,000 years to go through

Geothermal water gave Boise one of its claims to fame. Boise was the first city in the world to develop its geothermal resources as a major way of heating homes.

this cycle and come out of a tap in a Boise home.

Today, about 400 homes and eight major buildings are heated geothermally in Boise, at about half the cost of natural gas heating. Since 1892, an average of 700,000 gallons per day have been pumped during the heating season. Since 1981, the pumpage has

tripled, and 700,000 gallons per day are now being reinjected into the aquifer.

Boise's geothermics are a relatively small, confined system. But they are a part of the larger, more interesting phenomena of the Snake River Plain and one of our planet's biggest hot spots.

Northern Nevada and southern Idaho sit atop what geologists call "the Battle Mountain Heat Flow High." More heat flows out of the earth here than almost anywhere else, probably because of a large, shallow pool of hot magma just a few thousand feet down.

A portion of this geologic hot spot appears to have literally melted its way across southern Idaho as the North American continent slowly drifted over it, from east to west. Evidence for this includes the entire Snake River Plain, which describes an upside-down arc stretching from Oregon to Wyoming. The Plain is fairly flat, punctuated by "holes" at places like the Bruneau-Jarbridge Volcanics and the Craters of the Moon. Its present end is the Yellowstone region, where we find great geothermal activity and two of the largest volcanic calderas on earth: one in Yel-

lowstone National Park and the 20-mile diameter circular caldera of Idaho's Island Park.

Spencer Wood thinks earthly tectonics most likely explain the Plain's creation, but other geologists have suggested a more dramatic cause. They posit that a giant meteor may have struck southeastern Oregon about 17 million years ago, puncturing the earth's crust and creating the hot spot that subsequently caused the formation of the Snake River Plain.

For whatever reasons, Boise sits close above a pool of hot magma. But this situation poses little danger of new volcanoes or killer earthquakes. The cracks in the earth that help heat Boise's water are small and stable compared to other Idaho faults, like the one near Cascade or the one near Mt. Borah, which caused Idaho's last major earthquake, the 7.3 temblor of 1983.

Again, much of this area's dramatic earth activity happened when no one was here to see it. The first people in the valley were probably Ice Age elephant hunters, arriving more than 14,000 years ago. As the climate warmed they may have moved north with their quarry: elephants,

Above: *Frank Church-River of No Return Wilderness.*
Left: *Cold day and hot springs on the south Fork of the Payette.*

bison, camels and giant sloth. Or, as Twin Falls amateur archaeologist William Studebaker and others have suggested, Boise's first residents wandered southeast and became part of the prehistoric Mississippian Culture.

Their culture was replaced by a more varied hunter-gatherer tradition. Before 1600 A.D., local Shoshone peoples subsisted on deer, elk, buffalo, camas and seeds, and an abundance of salmon from the

---

Indians say that Castle Rock, rising above Boise's East End, is a sacred burial ground.

Snake and Boise rivers. Compared to some other Western Indians, Boise-area Shoshone could be called "primitive." They neither used organized agriculture, as did some tribes to the south, nor did they preserve their salmon by smoking it, as did the Nez Perce, just to the northwest. Their lifestyle matched the seasons—feast and famine—until the coming of the horse, and later the white people.

It can be said that the horse brought mobility to the Indians, and then the whites brought everything to a halt. The Boise Shoshone got the horse shortly after the Spanish settlement of New Mexico, around 1600 (200 years before the coming of the whites). The Shoshone were now able now to follow the buffalo, and other tribes were able to visit the Boise area. Nez Perces from the north, Paiutes from Nevada, Cheyennes from Colorado, and Crows from Wyoming, all gathered at a great *Sheewoki* trading fair, which took place for two months during salmon fishing season. The Boise area became a great center of commerce on an increasingly busy Indian trade route between the Great Plains and the Pacific.

Present-day Indians say that Castle Rock, rising above Boise's East End, is a sacred burial ground. The Kelly Hotsprings, to the east of the Natatorium, were an important wintertime spa. Perhaps the most impressive relic from the times of the Original Americans is Map Rock, located southwest of Boise near the Snake River. Map Rock's petrographs have been thought to be an Indian chart, showing the Snake River and much Northwest geography.

The Pacific Fur Company—

J.J. Astor's Astorians—were the first whites to see the Boise area, in 1811. It was these French trappers who first called this place "Boisée," meaning "wooded."

It was more than wooded, it was also full of beaver (as it is again today). And the area was so important that the Indians fiercely resisted establishment of white outposts. Only Marie Dorian and her children survived an 1814 massacre of John Reid's Hudson Bay Company party by Bannock Indians.

As the Indians resisted the Hudson's Bay Company, so did its Scotch and English trappers resist encroachments by American fur trappers coming over from the Rocky Mountains. Hudson's Bay tried for years to "trap out" the area, to keep the Americans from expanding into fur areas farther west. "The Company" finally established its Fort Boise, in 1834, at the confluence of the Boise and Snake rivers. The fort operated successfully until 1855.

Americans bound for Oregon's Willamette Valley had been passing through Boise since about 1840. "Passing through" was about all they wanted to do, but certainly, after the dry Snake River plains, the wooded Boise River must have looked beautiful. Most of the emigrants probably agreed with this 1832 account by Captain Benjamin Bonneville, as told by Washington Irving: "The country about the Boise (or Woody) River is extolled by Captain Bonneville as the most enchanting he had seen in the Far West, presenting the mingled grandeur and beauty of mountain and plain, of bright running streams and vast grassy meadows waving to the breeze."

Oregon's Willamette Valley was ready-made for settlement, offering temperate climate, abundant rainfall, and easy ocean access. The Boise Valley, on the other hand, had to be made ready for settlement. Bonneville's "grandeur" did more to whet the appetite then dull the hunger. Geographic isolation, hot-then-cold continental climate, and a flood-then-fail water supply provided plenty of drama but little promise. The emigrants rambled on through.

Little is left of the original Fort Boise, whose site can be reached from Highway 20, west of Parma. Little is left, too, of the Oregon Trail, which once ran down Main Street and whose wagon ruts can still be seen in several places, including at a BLM site off Black Creek Road, southeast of Boise. But the vista enjoyed by the Astorians and all the emigrants can still be enjoyed from the rimrock just east of the city, by anyone who stands with the desert to her back, the mountains to her right, and the green valley spreading before her. Perhaps a better and more poignant viewpoint is one certainly used by the Indians: the overlook at Table Rock.

The Indians had Boise pretty much to themselves for six short years, until George Grimes' party discovered gold in the Boise Basin, on August 2, 1862. Then it was, "Katy, bar the door." Thousands of miners arrived before Christmas. Idaho became a U.S. Territory in 1863. Southwest of Boise, Silver City sprang up. For a short time, Idaho City, just northwest of Boise, was the biggest town in the Northwest. All these miners needed to eat. The future site of Boise was lower, more sheltered, and easily irrigated. A "farm rush" soon followed the gold rush.

Boise was the right place at the right time. Gold and silver strikes occurred to the north, south and east. The Oregon emigrant trail ran east and west. The U.S. Army wanted a regional fort for protection against Indians. And crops grew well, where these interests transected.

The effect of standing here to watch the full moon rise is chilling, stirring, and wonderful.

Boise seemed to grow from a place, to a fort, to a town, in a matter of days. Major Pinckney Lugenbeel laid the logs for the U.S. Army's Fort Boise on July 6, 1863. The new town was platted, the very next day. A sense of this time can be got in a few hours, by first viewing still cottonwoody Government Island (where Pinckney camped before establishing the fort), then visiting the log cabin preserved on Fort Street near the Federal Building, then walking through the Military Reserve graveyard, just up Mountain Cove Road, where soldiers and early Boise citizens rest.

Idaho the Undiscovered

Peregrine falcon.

Facing page, top: *Bruneau Sand Dunes State Park.*
Bottom: *Three Island Crossing.*

Seattle folk might call Idaho "Washington's best kept secret." And Montanans might value Idaho as a vast buffer against California. But for much of the nation, Idaho could as well be called "I-*dun-no*." And protective *Idunnoans* might like to keep it that way.

Idaho was the last of present-day states to be "discovered" by Europeans. It is the only state for which Lewis and Clark could be called the first explorers. And their expedition was guided, in part, by someone who already knew the country. She was Sacajawea—a native Idahoan.

Even the intrepid Lewis and Clark needed two running starts to get through rugged Idaho. In 1805 they came over the Continental Divide from what later would be Montana and dropped into the Salmon River country. The wild and free Salmon River forms a priceless bloodline, a splendid song line, a line of credit at the bank of the soul. It opens and empties the purest part of the natural heart of America—a heart that beats with the thunder of falling water.

Meriwether Lewis and William Clark wanted to boat the Salmon in order to get to the Pacific. But according to Sacajawea's people the Salmon deserved its future title, The River of No Return. They warned Lewis and Clark that the canyon was impassable, and that the country toward Boise was incredibly rugged.

One Indian told them that "for the first seven days we should be obliged to climb over steep and rocky mountains" inhabited by "a fierce and warlike nation...called the broken mockersons...who lived like the bear of other countries among the rocks," and that "in passing this country the feet of our horses would be so much wounded with the stones many of them would give out."

These "broken mockerson" people may have been the Sheepeater Indians, who inhabited the mountain fastness to Boise's northeast.

The Indian then described the Craters of the Moon as a place "in which we must suffer if not perish," and went on to mention what may have been the Boise Valley as "a country tolerable fertile and partially covered with timber."

William Clark attempted to

float the Salmon River anyway. Afterwards, he wrote: "the passage…with canoes is entirely impossible, as the water is Confined between huge Rocks and the Current beeting from one against another… Every man appeared disheartened from the prospects of the river."

Central Idaho was the only

In many ways, Idaho does represent some of America's biggest, best, and precious last.

geography that stopped the explorers. Lewis and Clark backtracked into Montana, and tried Idaho again farther north. There, they faced the second most rugged portion of their journey, although Lewis noted that they were "proceding on through a beautiful country."

Idaho, like its famed Salmon River, is a visual and spiritual *rush*. "Idaho is what America was," Idahoans like to say. And, in many ways, Idaho does represent some of America's biggest, best, and precious last.

Idaho's Salmon River is the last, biggest undammed river system left in the contiguous U.S. It flows through an enormous wilderness and through the biggest chunk of granite on the continent, the monstrous Idaho batholith. Then, the Salmon joins the Snake River in North America's deepest gorge. People now call this Hells Canyon, but the French fur trappers called it *la maudite rivière enragée*, the cursed, furious river. The Indians were more poetic. They called Hells Canyon "the place of the last jumping off."

Idaho has been a challenge to more than geographers, to others besides Lewis and Clark. Idaho is a challenge, just to describe. The most "mountained" of the 50 states, and the wildest of the lower forty-eight, Idaho pushes a wedge of over 80 named mountain ranges south out of Canada along the west slope of the Continental Divide. Sixty-four percent of Idaho is federal lands; 40 percent (more than any other state) is National Forest. Less than one-half percent is urban or built-up; less than 15 percent is agricultural; 85 percent *looks* wild. According to the Wilderness Society,

almost 14 million acres—one quarter of the state—is existing wilderness, with less than a third of that protected.

From Canada to Nevada, Pacific Northwest forests of cedar and larch transition to Northern Rockies tracts of fir, spruce and pine and then to Great Basin stands of juniper, piñon and sage, and vast volcanic deserts.

Idaho's Panhandle North is a deep water, deep forest, deep green country, with some of the biggest freshwater lakes around. Priest, Pend Oreille, and Coeur d'Alene lakes abound with trophy trout. Lake Pend Oreille is so deep and secretive that the U.S. Navy uses it to test submarines. The Purcell and the Cabinet mountains hide lynx, moose, grizzly bear, and the nation's only herd of woodland caribou.

In spring, the road south from Coeur d'Alene to Lewiston seems to wind through a hundred-mile-long golf course. Fairways of rapeseed and wheat fields are bordered by roughs of pine and fir. South of Lewiston, the road climbs through the Nez Perce Indian Reservation onto the Camas Prairie, where rich, black dirt grows abundant wheat. At White Bird Hill the highway suddenly drops into the Salmon River gorge, where Nez Perce chieftains White Bird and Joseph first fought the U.S. Army, in 1877, and the Nez Perce began their heroic, 1,500-mile march into tragedy.

This section of the Salmon River gives a glimpse of the great wildness on either side of the canyon. Place names and landmarks give hints of the ruggedness: He Devil, She Devil, Purgatory, Whangdoodle and Dead Mule Peak. As the pioneers would say, "This is country with the bark still on!"

The Salmon River divides Idaho, north and south, and it unites the great wilderness areas, home to bighorn, mountain goat, elk, cougar and wolf. Except perhaps during hunting season, you can walk—or ski—here for weeks on end, and never see another human being.

Long tied to the seesaw economics of timber, minerals and agriculture, Idaho is now on a financial roll. Timber and agriculture are doing well and cities in each section of the state are booming. Boise is a governmental and high-tech industry center with an enviable quality of life. Sandpoint, Coeur d'Alene, McCall and Sun Valley are all meccas for tourists and magnets for newcomers seeking the good life. And Idaho Falls serves as headquarters for the Idaho National Engineering Laboratory. That bearded desert rat seen hiking the sand dunes is likely to be a nuclear physicist.

Unfortunately, many smaller communities are losing their young people to careers in the bustling city. But the small-town West feeling is

For most Americans, Idaho remains undiscovered. For many Idahoans, it should remain unspoken.

alive—even in Boise—and the embracing geography is such a powerful influence that it tends to turn most Idahoans into small-town western types: quiet, conservative, and tolerant.

Idaho's mountains make people feel both isolated and free, while their inspiring perspectives make people creative. As the "rock house artist," Salmon River Dick, says in a William Studebaker poem:

I don't think I ever decided.
I just started building out of rock.
Not because there were so many
but because they were arranged so bad.

Idaho's population has only recently passed 1 million, and its nationally known artistic output is slight. Poet Ezra Pound was born near Ketchum and novelist Marilyn Robinson comes from Sandpoint. Both left Idaho to do their work elsewhere.

Ernest Hemingway moved to Idaho toward the end of his life, and he ended his life in Ketchum. His suicide may seem a strange way to end a description of the state. But, if you think of Hemingway and his spare, clear, strong prose, you might understand why he finished it all here.

For most Americans, Idaho remains undiscovered. For many Idahoans, it should remain unspoken.

Left: The 1993 Sesquicentennial Wagon Train nears Boise. *Below:* Kathryn Albertson Park in fall attire.

Facing page: "Broken Mockerson" country—the rugged Middle Fork of the Salmon.

This cemetery could be called "Boise's Boot Hill." The effect of standing here to watch the full moon rise is chilling, stirring, and wonderful.

While other Northern Rocky Mountain start-up

So Boise had the capital, but with neither officials nor money.

towns were filled with young male "boomers," Boise immediately became a family town of merchants supplying the gold camps. About 12 percent of Idaho's women and children lived in Boise, which had only two percent of the Territory's entire population. A school was established in Boise that first winter.

By 1864, Boise seemed to have secured a future in transportation, mining, lumbering, business, and agriculture. But it lacked political might. A temporary territorial capital had been established at Lewiston, which served a large mining district that had just gone bust. Ninety percent of Idaho's population now lived in the Boise area, and

the pack trail to Lewiston was often impassable. Boise legislator Henry Riggs managed to have Boise designated the permanent capital, something that Idaho Governor Caleb Lyon liked just fine, but which his fellow Lewistonians did not like at all.

Caleb Lyon then said he was going out duck hunting, and he left Lewiston, never to return. All Lewiston now had left for a political pedigree were some records and the territorial seal. Lewiston authorities mounted a 24-hour guard. Finally, the Territorial Secretary used a U.S. Army detachment from Fort Lapwai to overwhelm the guard, and Boise got the capital goods.

Boise also got Caleb Lyon for just long enough to suffer his further shenanigans. He helped lose other people's money in schemes promising railroads, steamboat lines, Owyhee Mountain diamonds, and the exploitation of freed slaves in Idaho gold mines. In 1866, Lyon finally went away for good, with all of Idaho's Indian funds. This was soon after a colleague had spirited away the entire Territorial treasury.

So Boise had the capital, but with neither officials nor money. To make matters

worse, the Legislature was full of ex-Confederate Democrats, refugees from the recent Civil War. The next governor, a Radical Republican, refused to pay the Democrats with money he did not have, and for the second time in three years, Idaho's government had to be assisted by a detachment of U.S. soldiers, these from Fort Boise.

But Boise persisted—as the supply center for mining activity, as the military center for U.S. Army Indian campaigns, and as a good place to raise a family. In 1869, Tom Davis began harvesting from the 7,000 fruit trees in his orchard that would later become Julia Davis Park. Boise then had 400 buildings, including 250 homes, four elementary schools, two churches, and 20 saloons. Those saloons are all gone, but St. Michael's Episcopal Church, built at Seventh and Bannock in 1866, still graces the city from its riverside location near Broadway on the BSU campus. Across the river, in Julia Davis Park, Thomas Logan's 1865 adobe house has been beautifully restored. A few blocks away, on Grove Street between Sixth Street and Capitol Boulevard, stands Cyrus Jacobs' 1864 little brick house, now a Basque museum.

During the last three decades of the 19th century, Boiseans extended irrigation canals to areas away from the river bottom, developed the world's first extensive geothermal water system, started construction on the capitol, and finally got a branch rail line to come all the way into town. An electric streetcar system was started, only two years after one began in New York City.

And Boise dodged another political bullet. North Idaho wanted to rejoin Washington Territory, and some Congressmen wanted to attach southern Idaho to Nevada. Their efforts were thwarted, and on July 4, 1890, Idaho became a state. Boise's population doubled that same year, to 4,000 residents.

Beautiful remnants of this era include the U.S. Assay Office on Main Street, the Territorial Penitentiary and Bishop's House at the Old Penitentiary grounds, and some of the fine houses on Warm Springs Avenue.

After 1900, two impressive cathedrals—St. Michael's Episcopal and St. John's Roman Catholic—and the elegant Idanha Hotel were serving the public. The Owyhee

Hotel opened in 1910, and the state capitol dome was completed in 1912.

These buildings and others provided the stages for much early Boise drama and democracy. Clarence Darrow stayed at the Idanha during the famous Big Bill Haywood conspiracy trial. Will Rogers enjoyed Boise's humorous place names, specifically the "Idanha-ha" and "Owyhee-hee" hotels, both in the capital of "Idaho-ho."

Boise continued to grow and modernize at a remarkable pace for a city so far from everywhere else. Population grew from 8,000 in 1900 to 20,000 by 1910. Then the population stabilized, while Boise consolidated. Developers and promoters worked to expand irrigation and to attract the Union Pacific's main line to Boise. Then, as when the state capital came to Boise, a lot happened fast.

This time, what was happening was transportation. Main-line passenger train service began in 1925, long after that of many other cities. But regular air mail flights began in 1926, and Boise was among the nation's first cities with regular airline service. Motorbuses replaced Boise's electric trolleys in 1928.

Boise missed much of the expansive "Roaring Twenties," because of its dependence on unprofitable agriculture. But Boiseans were able to join the entire country in the Great Depression of the '30s and early '40s.

As a governmental center, however, Boise benefited from

Maybe it's better to call it, "a great metropolitan heart."

the large federal programs of the New Deal. It solidified its position as the national government's clearing house to a great rural area, a position it still holds today.

Two enterprises begun during the Great Depression and World War II still benefit Boise. Boise State University began as an Episcopal Church junior college in 1932, and was moved to the grounds of a Boise airfield across the river from Julia Davis Park, in 1939. The precursor to the current Boise Air Terminal began the next year as a U.S. Army bomber training facility. Military activity at the airport provided stability for Boise while many of its young

Julia Davis Park.

Several Idaho-born businesses were growing steadily as well, including Morrison-Knudsen, J.R. Simplot, Idaho First National Bank (now West One), Boise Cascade, Ore-Ida Foods, and Trus-Joist (now TJ International). These enterprises now form part of the Boise's substantial corps of national and multinational corporations.

Boise tried to self-destruct in the 1970s, with a massive demolition of buildings south of Main Street. Fortunately, less evidence of that destruction remains every year. And Boise succeeds, sometimes in spite of itself. Corporate expertise, combined with amazing largess from wealthy Boise families and remarkable volunteerism, has helped Boise grow in other ways as well—especially in cultural and physical amenities. These include a marvelous system of riverside parks connected by the beautiful Greenbelt; the fine ski area at Bogus Basin, just above town; the Morrison Center for the Performing Arts; and other urban and natural improvements that make Boise what it is today.

Boise is now "growing like Topsy" again, with the large Towne Square mall anchoring retail development in West

people were away at war. And the G.I. Bill provided a boost for Boise Junior College after the war was over.

Several wonderful buildings from the '20s and '30s remain to delight Boiseans—including the 1927 Egyptian Theater, with its odd, outside-inside combination Spanish-Egyptian motif and its big pipe organ, installed just before the advent of "talkies"; the 1930 art deco Hotel Boise (now the Hoff Building); and the beautiful Spanish clock tower of 1925 Union Pacific depot, which Morrison-Knud-

sen Co. has lovingly refurbished and proudly renamed. Structural beams from Boise's "College Field" airport now support a shelter's roof in Kathryn Albertson Park.

After World War II, the Boise area grew steadily, rising from 40,000 people in 1940, to 50,000 in 1950, to 70,000 in 1960. In 1958, Boise built its second public high school—Borah High—after a fortunately unsuccessful attempt by some to build a single, gigantic high school on the grounds of the present Ann Morrison Park.

Above: Boise's Greenbelt is the skier's "great white way."
Below: Ballet Idaho, live at the Morrison Center.

Boise, the Park Center corporate campus on the river east of Broadway Avenue, and many new, mostly upscale housing developments—to the west, along the river, in the foothills, and on a bluff to the southeast. Downtown's future looks great along Main Street, and oddly vacant one block to the north. But several planned developments on Idaho Street should rejuvenate that portion of town.

Indeed, from Park Center to the state capitol, there seems to be evolving a vibrant corporate-educational-cultural-retail-restaurant-governmental core. That's a big mouthful. Maybe it's better to call it, "a great metropolitan heart."

Dry Country Garden

Spring skiing is terrific in March, but along the Greenbelt the buds are popping, and Boiseans flood the parks and bikeways.

Places often get their names from what is different about them. And the French explorers didn't call this area *Boisée* because it was more of the same. *La Rivière Boisée* means "the wooded river." Early visitors were delighted to see the green woods and the always-flowing water in this oasis at the edge of a desert.

Aridity is the climate factor that most affects Boise's character. It accounts for the color of the lands surrounding the valley, the earth tones of yellows, browns, sage and purple. The cool blue-green summits of the Boise Mountains are colored blue-green *because* they are cool. Their heights chill more rain out of the passing clouds, and that helps the fir and pine forest make its mountaintop stand.

Some Boiseans say that if you don't like the weather, wait a few minutes—it'll change. But, in fact, Boise's weather is among the nation's mildest, considering its 2,700-foot elevation, its latitude as far north as Portland, Maine, and its landlocked geographic location. The National Weather Service describes Boise's climate as "dry and temperate, with sufficient variation to be stimulating." Nearly ev-

ery day is tolerable, and many are delightful.

Moist air masses from the North Pacific are often drained by coastal mountains before they reach Boise. Thus, clear, sunny weather rules the summers. One-hundred-degree days occur nearly every year, but really hot periods rarely last long, and are blessedly accompanied by low humidity. July is the hottest month, with a normal high of 91° and a sleepable low of 59°. Boise's record high is 111°, set in July of 1960.

On average, it doesn't freeze in Boise between early May and early October. Early autumn is bright and idyllic. Late autumn is often gray and damp. In winter, the usual northwest airflow alternates with warm wet storms from the direction of Baja, and with occasional Arctic blasts straight down out of Canada. Cold snaps with low temperatures of 10° or lower often last longer than summer heat waves, but there is rarely much wind to add to the chill. January is the coldest month, with a normal high of 37° and a low of 23°. Boise's record low is -25°, set in December of 1990.

Boiseans prefer just enough storms to blow out temperature inversions, which fair weather/high pressure systems sometimes cause in the valley. While these inversions often trap pollutants in the valley and create what Boiseans like least about their city's climate, the accompanying "Rocky Mountain Highs" make for beautiful skiing at Bogus Basin—14 miles north and 5,000 feet above town.

Spring skiing is terrific in March, but along the Greenbelt the buds are popping, and Boiseans flood the parks and bikeways. March winds can be raw, but by May the soft air carries the scents of cottonwood and sage, and the long spring evenings are lovely.

Precipitation averages 12 inches a year, with January heaviest at 1.64 inches, and July driest at a quarter of an inch. The biggest one-day rain fell in June of 1958, with 2.24 inches. In recent years, 1983 saw the most precipitation, with nearly 19 inches. In all of 1992, only 7.65 inches fell, and this after five years of drought. The year 1993 seemed to have reversed the trend: 10 inches had fallen by the first week of June.

Prevailing winds average 8 to 10 m.p.h. out of the southeast, except in summer, when they tend from the northwest.

The greatest wind gust measured 71 m.p.h., in July of 1987. Tornadoes and ice storms are practically unknown. Short dust storms sometimes accompany a dry cold front. Thunderstorms occur mainly during spring and summer. These are rarely severe, but neighboring forests and grasslands are often set ablaze. In the summer of 1992, Boiseans watched for months as the nearby Foothills Fire grew and grew. Before autumn rains finally quenched it, the Foothills Fire charred one-quarter million acres.

Much of the precipitation that falls in Boise falls in the winter when plants do not grow. Summers are generally as dry as a skillet, and as hot. Boise Valley looked like a living emerald to the early explorers because yearly spring floods watered the cottonwoods. The valley presents a green summer haven today because of the man-made rain of irrigation.

In the past, irrigation and its promise of agricultural riches drove many a dream and scheme. It is still a jewel of an idea. Let precipitation fall as snow in the winter and be held in deposit in the mountains until spring. Then

catch it as runoff water in reservoirs behind dams, and sluice it down canals to farm fields. That takes care of the problem of summer aridity, and takes advantage of the abundant summer sun. Add turbines to the dams to generate electricity and then use that power to light up Boise and run well-pumps to irrigate more acreage.

Boise irrigators began mov-

March winds can be raw, but by May the soft air carries the scents of cottonwood and sage, and the long spring evenings are lovely.

ing off the river bottoms after 1876, when a flood moved the river's main channel. In 1878, William B. Morris opened a seven-mile canal onto the bench. Because of financial troubles, much more development was delayed until 1906, when Diversion Dam began supplying the New York Canal. In 1907, Arrowrock Dam was begun. It stood as the highest dam in the world when it was finished in 1916.

47

The Idaho International Women's Challenge—
among the best women's bicycle races in the
world.

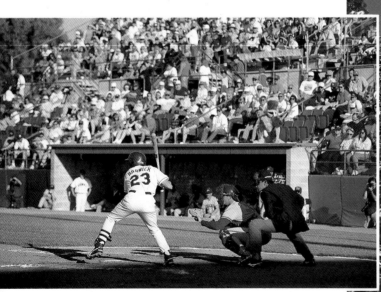

Above: The Boise Hawks professional ball club
nurtures rookie talent for the California
Angels.
Right: Alpine skiing at Bogus Basin.

Lucky Peak and Anderson Ranch impounded more Boise River water for irrigation, and lessened the threat of floods.

Getting water to crops was everything to many early Boiseans. Boise even had a semi-pro baseball team called the Irrigators back in 1911. This team name won out over several competitors, such as Kangaroos, Mutts, and Convicts. Following similar agricultural themes, Parma fielded the Plum Pickers. Emmett sponsored the Melon Eaters. Mountain Home, which had earlier gone by the name of Rattlesnake, showed a different sensibility, calling its team the Dudes.

Nowadays, even as the metropolitan area swells to displace the rich farmland west of the city, the Boise area still accounts for major crop production and contributes mightily to Idaho's economy. In all, Idaho ranks among the top five U.S. producers of potatoes, trout, prunes and plums, dry peas, lentils, sugar beets, barley, dry beans, mint, hops, onions, and sweet cherries. Southern Idaho produces some very fine wines and leads the nation in the production of trout. Six Boise-area counties account for 28 percent of Idaho's agricultural product, for a value of $641 million. Even highly urbanized Ada County still has one-quarter million acres of farm land.

The harnessing of rivers has changed the color of the land and brought agricultural wealth to the Boise. But of course, nothing is free, not even rainwater and gravity. Boise's main reservoirs—Arrowrock, Lucky Peak, and Anderson Ranch—take away precious wintering range from big game herds (as does the city itself). And downstream dams on the Snake River and below have abolished any natural return of salmon and steelhead to their historical spawning beds in Boise. The environmental and economic trade-offs caused by damming Northwest rivers are difficult to determine, but they are undoubtedly large.

Still, the water keeps flowing for the benefit of Boise.

And Boise exists as an agricultural and urban oasis in a dry land of few people. The wishful slogan, "rain follows the plow," never held true for the American West. But, in Boise's case, the plow did follow the new irrigation canals, and more immigrants followed the plow. And more people keep coming until we have the metropolis of Boise today.

Irrigation and agriculture are Southwest Idaho's economic backbone, as well as the fountainhead for much western culture. The Boise area produces far more than

> *Boise exists as an agricultural and urban oasis in a dry land of few people.*

crops and beef. It produces a national treasure: cowboys, cowgirls and farmers. And they also reflect a way of life and a work ethic that continue today. In her book, *A Victorian Gentlewoman in the Far West*, author Mary Hallock Foote wrote this about the engineers building the Boise canals: "...often I thought of one their phrases, 'The angle of repose,' which was too good to waste on rockslides or heaps of sand. Each one of us in the Cañon was slipping and crawling and grinding along seeking what to us was that angle, but we were not any of us ready for repose."

Left: Jim Gael sculpts "The King" at the McCall Winter Carnival.
Far left: "Mutton busting" at the Snake River Stampede in Nampa.

Facing page, top: Horse racing at Les Bois track.
Bottom: A McCall winter.

Diversion Dam above Boise helps water the valley.

Neighborhoods & Nature

Garnet Monnie says that her northwest Boise neighborhood owns a quality common to many Boise neighborhoods: the feeling of open country. "The people who live in the neighborhood try really hard to maintain that country feeling."

Garnet Monnie tends thousands of flowers in the neighborhood nursery established by her grandfather, many years ago. Geothermal water heated beneath Boise for thousands of years warms the family greenhouses below the 1905 homestead on Hill Road.

In the 1920s and 1930s, Thomas Edwards was called "The White Chinaman" because he competed with the Chinese truck gardens along the Boise River. His granddaughter Garnet grew up with her hands in the earth-warmed dirt and holds strong feelings about nature and place.

She said her northwest Boise neighborhood remains a great place to raise kids. This part of Boise, though long established, owns a quality common to many Boise neighborhoods: the feeling of open country. Monnie said, "The people who live in the neighborhood try really hard to maintain that country feeling." Indeed, many newer Boise neighborhoods—and older ones like Monnie's—feel distinctly *horsy*. Often there is a horse in a nearby pasture, and even the new developments are frequently built around old farm homes and ranch houses, which conserve the agrarian setting.

And while many Boise neighborhoods have a cowboy feel to them, the very oldest neighborhoods—the North and East ends—still protect an earlier, *pioneer* ambiance, with touches of antiquity like stone carriage steps and the ancient testaments of the old homes themselves. The oldest neighborhoods share with some of the newest a working relationship with wildness.

Boise's first-settled districts maintain the city's best contacts with nature, because of their nearness to both river and hills. East Boise, for example, cannot be beat for its immediate access to the unencumbered outdoors. Mike and Deb Weber and their two young daughters live in a new, secluded neighborhood between Warm Springs Avenue and the Boise River. When they leave home in the morning, the loudest sound they hear is the river across the street. They often take Carmen and Katie to skip rocks and watch wildlife. And that's just the Greenbelt, which is sometimes "too crowded," said Mike. Within one mile of their home, Mike and Deb can jog or bike Castle Rock and Table Rock, and rise far above the city. From there, it's often tempting to keep going—to head up Rocky Canyon to Aldape Summit and the forested ridge, or to continue past Table Rock to the open bluffs over the Lucky Peak reservoir cliffs.

Both Deb and Mike are Race to Robie Creek veterans. They enjoy the camaraderie of the 2,000 runners who brave Aldape and beyond, but they say that if you really want to run the Boise hills alone, try the very same route the day after the race. It's just you and the birds, and perhaps a few ghosts trying to catch their breaths.

The Silak-Miller family lives near the Webers' newer home, in an 85-year-old Warm Springs Avenue house, heated by natural hot water. They love the old place. Cathy Silak said, "You can feel the texture of the past. We found some 1912 school attendance slips in an old desk."

She added, "[The geothermal heat is] toasty and pervasive. In winter, we regulate the heat by opening and closing windows."

Warm Springs Avenue is Boise's oldest existing address of prestige. The earliest was Grove Street, which from the 1860s was the shady abode of Boise's "best" families. Warm Springs Avenue took over the title in 1892, when C.W. Moore's family moved into their new mansion on the corner of Walnut and Warm Springs. They hooked up to Boise's natural hotsprings water and made their home the first house in America heated by geothermal energy.

The stately Moore mansion is not the oldest on the avenue. That distinction belongs to the G.W. Russell house, at 1035 Warm Springs Avenue, built on the original Russell homestead, in 1868.

The Russell children had miles of open country to run and play in. Surprisingly, children growing up on Warm Springs today still have ready access to the great outdoors. The backyards of many homes maintain a rustic character. The C.W. Moore house still has a pasture behind it. The city's arboretum, Municipal Park, the Greenbelt and the MK Nature Center all lie a short stroll from Warm Springs. And at the east end of the avenue, at the Old Penitentiary, undeveloped open country climbs into the hills.

Boise second historic neighborhood is equally charming. The Harrison Boulevard Historic District, known by all as the "North End," extends from downtown north to the foothills. Harrison Boulevard itself has a stately feeling, not unlike Warm Springs, and benefits from a grassy center parkway. But the North End as a whole does not make one think of power and prestige. Rather, it evokes a long history of families, and a wonderful mix of incomes, occupations, and eccentricities. It may be hard to imagine, but Harrison Boulevard was the original place for teenagers to "cruise."

Boise's North End is a showplace of architecture, and it displays some of the best works of two of Boise's most accomplished architects: Tourtelotte and Hummell. A listing of North Ender architectural styles includes: Cottage, Bungalow, Frame, Colonial, Tudor, Art Moderne, Georgian, Queen Anne, Innovative Vernacular, California Mission, Clapboard, Salt Box, Colonial Revival, French Country, Cape Cod, Victorian, Half-Timber, and Stucco. And those are just the basic styles; several North End homes are combinations of several of the above, and at least two beauties were ordered right out of the old Sears mail order catalog.

First platted in 1891, and at times home to many of Boi-

se's best known citizens—including J.R. Simplot, William Agee, and Harry Morrison—Harrison Boulevard and the North End have also been home to a diverse group of people. Occupational listings for Harrison Boulevard residents have not changed drastically over the years. For example, "High White Collar" occupations accounted for 12.3 percent of residents in 1927, and 17.4 percent in 1965. "High Blue Collar" occupations accounted for 8.8 percent in 1927, and 6.2 percent in 1965. The Boulevard itself has seen more gentrification since 1965, but the entire North End is still a delightful mix of occupations and families.

Other Boise neighborhoods are distinguished by their geographies. Each bench has a long row of houses making use of the panoramas afforded. The rapidly developing Foothills provide stunning vistas. Upscale riverside neighborhoods combine nature and new styles, and many lower-income developments have access to the Greenbelt.

One of Boise's newest neighborhoods, Columbia Village, perches on a bench above the Boise River, so that

Above: *Sharing habitat in Boise.*
Top: *Race to Robie Creek—the ruggedest race loved by so many.*

the Villagers can drop down onto the Greenbelt or head eastward, along the old Oregon Trail, into the great expanse of public lands administered by the Bureau of Land Management.

Developer Al Marsden said the Columbia Village philosophy is "to create a community where we provide for all the needed facilities. It is a neighborhood, but it's not built piece-by-piece." Already, on weekends, 5,000 kids are playing on the 20 soccer fields and 12 baseball diamonds in Columbia Village's 160-acre sports park. Plans call for ten other parks and recreation centers, and ten miles of bike path, connecting with Boise's system. For all its amenities, Columbia Village is not an exclusive development. Homes will range in price from about $65,000 to about half a million dollars.

While Boiseans work hard to keep nature near their neighborhoods, they also think hard about the "nature" of neighborhoods. They ask, *What makes a neighborhood?* and, *What does it take to keep a neighborhood neighborly?* These days, when both spouses work and young children go to daycare, neighborhoods can be plenty empty at noontime. But "Neighborhoods, not subdivisions!" is a Boise rallying cry, emphasizing a continuing effort to make sure every new housing development comes fully to life and is fully livable, with parks, schools, a safe traffic flow, and easy access to nature.

City of Parks

The Boise Greenbelt creates such a tremendous natural attraction that Idahoans who live outside of Boise—in the high and wintry countryside—come to the Big City in the early spring, to more comfortably enjoy Mother Nature.

A strange thing occurred in the 1960s. Boiseans undertook the reversal of the Boise River. They didn't intend to make the river flow uphill, just to reverse the river's unfortunate trend: to take it from getting worse to getting better. In 1968, most of the river bank lay abused and derelict, littered with rusted car bodies and avoided by most Boiseans. By 1993, the Boise River Greenbelt had become a necklace of eight beautiful, marvelous parks strung together by 19 miles of lovely pathways, gracing both banks of the river. Boiseans now stroll, bike and skate these pathways, unbothered by auto traffic. The Boise Greenbelt creates such a tremendous natural attraction that, perhaps for the first time, Idahoans who live outside of Boise—in the high and wintry countryside—come to the Big City in the early spring, to more comfortably enjoy Mother Nature.

The Greenbelt is Boise's living symbol of pride. And it's this river running through the city that people say makes Boise the best. Animals find it attractive, as well. Although humanity now inhabits most of the prime bottomlands, the City of Boise provides important habitat for bald eagles, owls, songbirds and waterfowl, as well as beaver, muskrat, squirrel, deer, fox, and raccoon. Moose, bobcats and bear have visited the city in recent years. Magpies often escort joggers past the previous night's work of the beaver.

The Greenbelt pathway begins at Discovery State Park, near the spillway of Lucky Peak Dam, and travels through a dramatic canyon to Barber Flat, and then to Barber Park where in summer Boiseans put into the river by the thousands—in inner tubes, rafts, kayaks and canoes. From Barber, the pathway follows the old railroad line under the bluff of Warm Springs Mesa, through the middle of Warm Springs Golf Course, and past the Natatorium hotsprings swimming pool. It then goes through Municipal Park, skirts the MK Nature Center, and tunnels under the Broadway Avenue bridge.

At Broadway, Greenbelters can cross the river and follow the south bank back upstream, passing the Idaho Shakespeare Festival, the Park Center corporate campus, and several new neighborhoods. At River Run, the pathway changes from asphalt to sand as it enters a tranquil wildlife area, where bike riding is not allowed.

Downstream from Broadway, the pathway follows both banks. Three "no auto" bridges allow pedestrian crossing. On the north, the Greenbelt goes through Julia Davis Park, which began in the 1860s as an orchard of one of Boise's founders. Julia Davis now offers shady tranquillity, a boating lagoon, and a rose garden of 2,200 plants with 300 varieties. It is also the site of Zoo Boise, the Idaho State Museum, the Boise Art Museum, a family amusement park, and the Discovery Center for Science. Across Capitol Boulevard from Julia Davis Park, the Greenbelt passes the City Library and then continues on, under the Main Street Bridge and through Veteran's Park—with its many fishing holes—to the large Willow Lane outdoor sports complex.

On the south bank, the Greenbelt skirts the campus of Boise State University and passes through the shadow of the Morrison Center for the Performing Arts It then ducks under Capitol Boulevard Bridge and enters the 153-acre Ann Morrison Park, given to the city in honor of the first wife of Boise industrialist Harry Morrison. Americana Boulevard divides Ann Morrison from Kathryn Albertson Park, given to the city by Kathryn and Joe Albertson.

Kathryn Albertson Park is Boise's newest big park, and certainly the loveliest and most naturally colorful. Its plant species represent much of Idaho's native vegetation, and its design is absolutely perfect. Joe and Kathryn Albertson meant this park to be an urban wildlife sanctuary, and it is more than that. It is a harmonious habitat, complete with balanced proportions of food, water, shelter and space. Off limits to bicycles and ball games, the park is also reserved for the if-not-yet-endangered, then certainly exasperated, human wildlife: the pensive walker and the nature watcher.

On the river's north shore, below Willow Lane, the Greenbelt remains fragmented. Sections exist on both sides of the river near the Glenwood Bridge. Plans call for continuing the river pathway to Eagle Island State Park, and ultimately beyond there to the Snake River.

These dreams will no doubt be realized.

All totaled, Boise has 55 parks, with over 1,500 acres. Everyone has his favorites. Quarry View Park is tucked under the natural ramparts of Castle Rock, whose layered composition reveals local geology. Camel's Back Park sits at the north end of 12th Street, against a fantastic sledding hill. It offers what must be the world's best pre-litigation-era playground

All totaled, Boise has 55 parks, with over 1,500 acres. Everyone has his favorites: Quarry View, Camel's Back, Milwaukee...

equipment. Milwaukee Park, at the intersection with Northview, has a fine swimming pool and acres of playing fields.

Jim Hall, Director of Boise Parks and Recreation, said managing the parks is "a

Left: *Mother and child along the Salmon River.*

Below: *The view from Table Rock.*

Aerial nursery in Park Center Pond.

Diversion Dam on the Greenbelt.

Perhaps Boise's greatest contribution to the preservation of the wild is by serving as the World Center for Birds of Prey for the Peregrine Fund— which works worldwide to save endangered birds.

blast," and "absolutely nuts." He believes improving and expanding the park system is critical to maintaining Boise's quality of life. But Boise attracts so many immigrants that the cost of new parkland is rapidly increasing.

Boiseans have always enjoyed the city's natural bounty without recourse to middlemen. They heed Walt Whitman's call not to "take things at second or third hand." But many Boiseans now take advantage of the city's several nature interpretive centers, which help a person get closer to the mysteries of life.

Most impressive is certainly the MK Nature Center, run by the Idaho Department of Fish and Game, on Walnut Street, next to the Greenbelt. Brought into being on what was first a garbage dump, then Braves Field, and most recently a gravel parking lot, the Nature Center now offers Boiseans a "mountain stream" equivalent to the great ocean aquarium on Monterey Bay in California. In the improbable space of a few riverside acres, a 500-foot mountain stream bubbles out of the granite into a cold alpine pool. It cascades first over the granite, then slows

through volcanics, and finally settles into farmland and a warm water pond. Along the way, it recreates several Idaho wildlife habitats with a stunning similitude which reveals these habitats to the public. Underwater windows allow visitors to watch almost every species of Idaho fish, from egg stage, through fry, to spawning adult. The "lunker" window, with its enormous trout, is one of the favorite attractions.

Everybody wants first to look through the windows, but they soon realize there is more here. As Center Superintendent Terry Thompson said, "This is a real stream." The Idaho Department of Fish and Game created the habitat and planted the biggest fish, but now the little ecosystem virtually runs itself. In a virtual "build it and they will come" scenario, both vertebrates and invertebrates have colonized the Nature Center. Ducks and geese frequent the ponds. Great blue heron fish for bass and trout. A mink has moved into the rocks near a snag. And every summer day, midges and mayflies hatch so punctually that "you can set your watch by them," according to Thompson. Some visitors have complained about the insect hatches, but Thompson can only smile and suggest that they visit at a different time of day.

Fish and Game habitat manager Stacy Gebhardt called on his long experience and vast love of nature to determine where to place every rock at the Nature Center. Boise High students worked hard to help build it. In the summer of 1993, an auditorium and interpretive building opened, featuring computer-aided interactive displays to teach Boiseans about nature.

The Idaho Department of Fish and Game has also helped to make Kathryn Albertson Park into another kind of "nature center." Urban wildlife biologist Bruce Hawk often takes groups on tours through the park to show them how much wild nature can be found inside the city.

Zoo Boise, in Julia Davis Park, is in a major expansion in the 1990s. The zoo has over 200 animals, representing 77 species, 23 of which are threatened or endangered. Many Boise families and groups "adopt" individual animals, and help in their care and feeding. The children's "petting zoo" allows thousands of city kids to touch real animals. And a glance around the parking lot will show how many visitors come from rural Idaho. Zoo Boise has 200,000 visitors annually.

A zoo may seem out of place in a state like Idaho, which in itself is an enormous wildlife preserve. But many of Zoo Boise's animals would never otherwise be seen by Boiseans, and these "encounters of the second kind," between humans and animals, help instill a conservationist ethic.

Perhaps Boise's greatest contribution to the preservation of the wild is by serving as the World Center for Birds of Prey for the Peregrine Fund—which works worldwide to save endangered birds. The rescue from extinction of the peregrine falcon is the Fund's most famous achievement, but other birds, such as the California condor and the Amazonian harpy eagle, also benefit from the Fund's hard work. The Velma Morrison Interpretive Center, on West Flying Hawk Lane, helps expand the World Center's mission as a scientific, environmental and educational force for good.

Not all of Boise's "nature museums" present living, breathing, *wild* nature. The beautiful Botanical Gardens near the Old Pen present more civilized cultivations. The Discovery Center for Science, next to Julia Davis Park on Myrtle Street, showcases physical nature: gravity, magnetism, chemistry, optics, sound, and more. At the Discovery Center, it's "hands on" and "hands in," in a physically involving learning environment.

Above: *Ben Hogan Golf Tournament at the Hillcrest Country Club.*
Left: *The Sysco Festive Spirit Walk & Run is part of the River Festival.*

__Right:__ First meeting, in Ann Morrison Park.
__Below:__ Indian Hot Springs along the Bruneau River.

High on the Wild

It is difficult to choose where to begin when describing Boise's backyard. Beyond the metro limits, but close to the city, beckon both forested and high desert wilderness, as well as world-class whitewater and fantastic skiing...

Boise and Boiseans are high on the wild. With so much great nature *inside* Boise, and with Boiseans so devoted to the city's natural gifts, you might expect little action beyond sight of town.

But look around Boise, and one of the first things you'll notice is that Boise is a city of *rigs*. Campers, RVs, and 4-wheel-drives. It can seem that in every other driveway loiters somebody's Urban Escape Vehicle, usually pointed nose-toward-the-street, gassed up and ready to roll.

All of that nature activity inside Boise—the greenbelting, the fishing, the nature watching and the rest—is merely the off-the-cuff, 10-minute stuff. These can be done at any spare hour, with little preparation or drive time. Even powder skiing at Bogus Basin is so close and convenient that many Boiseans consider it an in-town activity.

All these activities sometimes seems to exist for the sole purpose of keeping Boiseans in training for hitting the hills and for tracking the Idaho Outback.

It is difficult to choose where to begin when describing Boise's backyard. Beyond the metro limits, but close to the city, beckon both forested and high desert wilderness, as well as world-class whitewater and fantastic skiing, and a canyon that shelters the largest concentration of birds of prey in North America.

Lofty granite peaks, "cities" of rock, moonlike volcanics, blue-green forests, hundreds of lakes, Saharan sand dunes, mile-deep canyons, and pastoral expanses of farm, orchard, vineyard and pasture all lie within range of a daytrip. And although Boise itself forms the cultural hub of much of Idaho, nearby towns compete with a range of attractions, including the jet-set diversions at Sun Valley, the family-set fun of Stanley and McCall, the fiddle and jazz jamborees at Weiser and Sunny Slope, and the ghost town haunts of Idaho City and Silver City.

One might spin a compass and describe Boise's playground in terms of a 360° circuit. And even then, the activities change through the 365-day cycle of the year. So, it is probably best to begin with a favorite Boise activity and proceed by proximity and association.

Boise may be the whitewater capital of the country. Les

Floating through the city is one of Boise's favorite pastimes.

Payette Lake, at McCall.

Bechdel, whom *Outside* magazine called "the man who is whitewater," said, "Idaho has the lion's share of exciting, floatable rivers." These rivers offer a wide range of wetting experiences: the Owyhee's isolation, the Hells Canyon's depths, the Salmon's length, the Selway's excitement. The sensation of floating an Idaho wild river may best be described as "suspense with the bottom dropping out." And Boiseans regularly drop their bottoms into wild boats to ride the wild waters.

One of the best rivers, the Payette, runs a mere 40 minutes from town. After work, Boiseans frequently surf its standing waves during long summer evenings. The Payette provides the setting for the annual Whitewater Rodeo, and its several forks offer every kind of fast water fun—from jetboat rallies, to beer-drinking raft trips, to Class V rapids and mandatory pull-outs where kayakers are warned to "abandon all hope" if they consider going farther. The "Canyon" section of the South Fork of the Payette offers so much excitement that a floater's only complaint might be that she didn't have time to enjoy the scenery.

Two hours from Boise, to-wards the headwaters of the North Fork lies idyllic Long Valley and the town of Mc-Call. McCall hovers at 5,000 feet elevation in the Salmon River Mountains, on the south shore of Payette Lake, whose moraine marks the edge of a glacier that carved out the lake basin some 10,000 years ago.

Payette Lake is shaped like an upside-down broken heart, six miles long and 18 miles around. It reflects mountain, forest, snow and cloud. It is blue-black in summer, aspen-gold in fall, snow-white in winter, and pale pewter in spring as it warms toward its late April thaw. The town and summer homes line about half of its shore. The rest of the shore is white sand beach and forested parkland. Mc-Call enjoys a legend about "Sharlie," Payette Lake's much-reported, much-doubted monster. Sharlie, no doubt, has a logical explanation—perhaps two large otters ca-vorting in the waves. But who needs explanations when sun-light on dark water spangles the imagination?

Just northwest of the lake is the Brundage Mountain Ski Resort, which in winter offers deep powder snow. Cross-country enthusiasts of-ten ski from the mountaintop all the way back to town. There, horse-drawn sleighs jingle past the McCall Winter Carnival's gigantic snow sculptures, like Egypt's Great Sphinx, and the Seated Buddha.

The glacial aspect of the McCall area is striking. You can stand in the center of

The Payette River and its several forks offer every kind of fast water fun—from jetboat rallies, to beer-drinking raft trips, to Class V rapids and mandatory pull-outs where kayakers are warned to "abandon all hope."

town and see where glaciers scarred the granite above timberline, and gouged more basins for dozens of other lakes. McCall, like Boise, sits on the edge of the great Idaho Batholith, an enormous

Little Redfish Lake and the Sawtooth Mountains.

chunk of granite that extends into Montana. This batholith—and several volcanic regions, as well—forms the base rock for Idaho's greatest treasure: the largest U.S. wilderness, outside of Alaska.

Idaho's wilderness seems to go on forever. Nowhere else can you fly so high and see so far, and see no signs of man. It harbors elk, deer, moose, bighorn, mountain goat, wolf, and bear. Its Salmon River— "the River of No Return"—remains the last and largest undammed river system in the contiguous U.S., providing oceangoing salmon and steelhead with their farthest retreats from the sea. Wilderness sprawls all around Boise, and Boise is blessed by it.

The Boise River's headwaters lie in this wilderness, not far to the east, high in the Sawtooth Mountain National Recreation Area. The Sawtooths rise to above 11,000 feet, and offer so many beautiful lakes and majestic peaks that the area has been studied for national park status.

Although most Idahoans agree the Sawtooths possess the beauty required of a great park, many think national park designation would draw too many visitors. And Idahoans are of many minds when it comes to federal "protection." For many, the label "National Recreation Area" is already an attractive nuisance. Others even resent "Wilderness" designations. They'll tell you that any label that gets an area "colored pink on a map" dooms that area to change. Some environmental contrarians would rather see the establishment of large flight training ranges near Mt. Home Air Force Base, 30 miles southeast of Boise, because such a designation restricts incursions by humans.

Just over the Sawtooths from Boise lies Sun Valley, which Averill Harriman selected in 1936 to become America's first European-style ski resort. Then, it was reached almost exclusively by Union Pacific passenger trains, and it became famous as a playground for the famous. Now it has scheduled air service, and it's still a famous playground. The lavish second homes of celebrities and the out-of-state wealthy make it an out-of-Idaho experience for many Idahoans.

Right: Two methods of transportation in a state with few roads. Below: Camas Prairie dressed in wildflowers.

Idaho's "Sierra" exists side by side with water. Bruneau Sand Dunes State Park.

But Sun Valley is there for a reason, and the reason is skiing. Bald Mountain offers the some of the best all-around skiing in the world. And then there are the other amenities: climate, scenery, summer, and nearby wilderness.

The Boise River flows out of the Sawtooths and drops a mile as it flows toward the city. The North Fork's color is often a glacial, milky blue, similar to that of the rivers of British Columbia. The upper reaches of the Boise's forks are now protected from development, and thus saved for wildlife and low-impact recreation. Dams slack the lower forks, and the reservoirs behind the dams provide boating and fishing. Arrowrock, Anderson Ranch, and Lucky Peak reservoirs are heavily used.

Spread out through the Boise River basin is the great gold country, which funded Boise's early expansion. Atlanta, Idaho City, and a few other small settlements still scratch a living out of the earth, and out of the tourists who come for the history. Idaho City, which for a moment was the Northwest's biggest town, retains a wonderful pioneer personality, even as it grows as a Boise bedroom.

The swing around Boise to the south presents a dramatic change in geography and ecology. Where lands north of Boise latitude are rugged and wooded, to the south the world is rugged and open. And while place names north of Boise are often discouraging (Bogus Basin, Disappointment Creek, No Business Mountain), place names south of Boise latitude can be positively frightening. Consider the Malad ("sick") River, the Inside Desert, and the Craters of the Moon. Topographical maps sometimes show nothing but lava. "Water tank" can be a location of note. Some people avoid the Idaho desert, but it is a fragile and fractured jewel.

The Craters of the Moon National Monument is god-awful gorgeous. The geology overwhelms; the desolation humbles. In spring, bright wildflowers contrast the black lava. In winter, snow beautifies a frozen inferno. Cross-country skiing here is some of the weirdest and most impressive on earth. This must be what Antarctica is like.

The Gooding City of Rocks provides hallucinations in granite and a dreamscape that threatens disorientation. The Malad River Gorge and the Bruneau Canyon offer the biggest experiences one can fit into an afternoon. The Bruneau Sand Dunes offer a mini-Sahara—this one with water and wildlife. And the

Looking good and liking it at Sun Valley.

Owyhee Uplands present dramatic range of changes and perspectives. Llama rancher Cutler Umbach said, "[The Owyhees] are an amazing place. It's one micro-climate backed up against another." Some of Boise's "desert rats" eschew the northern forests for the opportunities offered just south of the city. The desert in spring is the prettiest place in the state.

Also in spring, the desert is the busiest. A few miles south of Boise, the Snake River Birds of Prey Area protects one-half million acres of habitat for the densest population of nesting raptors in North America. This "vertical environment" of cliffs and sky offers a dazzling display of falcons, hawks and eagles, stooping at speeds nearing 200 m.p.h.

It would be impossible to name all the wild attractions that ring the city of Boise. It would be unwise to mention many of them, because publicity would ruin their quiet. And it would be unkind to reveal many others, because they are still secrets of long-time Idahoans. Perhaps the best advice to a newcomer to Boise is to get into a car and drive. Pick a direction and head out in the morning. The day will surprise with delights. Idaho offers distance, hundreds of miles of distance, that will draw you out of yourself and expand your vision. It offers perspective, a prospector's outlook: the main chance, the clear vein, the fresh and candid angle. Finally, Idaho offers a psychological clarity: a widening, opening, atmospheric sensation that spreads all the way from Bear Lake to Priest Lake, and from the Owyhees to the Bitterroots. Boiseans, indeed, are high on the wild, and the wild sustains their spirits.

A Boise Album

*A well loved city must provide many things:
a gathering place of ideas for vitality and
debate; a crossroads of travelers for renewal
and change; and nature, abundant,
available and safe. Finally, it must keep
beautiful to keep its people's love.*

Above: *The old railway depot restored to its beauty by the Morrison-Knudsen Corporation.*

Moonrise over the Boise River.

Right: Bald eagle along the Greenbelt.
Below: A pack trip into the Sawtooths.

Right: Up from six bits, but still a tradition.
Below: Looking over home.

Left: Winter visitors.
Below: Trail Creek Lake
in the Sawtooth
Wilderness.

Above: *The beautiful change of season along the Boise River.*
Right: *The Salmon River is, as they say, "Fun for the whole family."*

Facing page: *Where the Boise River goes—Hells Canyon of the Snake.*

Capital Cultures

Idaho Indians on sacred ground, in Boise's Hull's Gulch.

Facing page, top left:
Internationally famous Gene Harris at home in Boise.
Top, right: *The Morrison Center for the Performing Arts, a finely tuned instrument.*
Bottom: *Idaho Shakespeare Festival—theater by the river.*

Explaining America gets harder and harder, as our nation grows more diverse. The statistics and qualities that describe our society seem to grow more complex by the year. *Who we are* depends a lot on who does the asking. Statistics are only part of the picture, but they give us framework to start from.

Statistically, Boiseans would seem a fortunate lot. They avoided the long recession of the late 1980s and early 1990s. Construction continues to boom. The average income of Boiseans remains high for Idaho, and about average for the U.S. as a whole. Boise's crime rate is low for a city of its size. The environment is for the most part enviable in its cleanliness, and the area's climate is healthful. The city has two regional medical centers, providing a redundant health resource for Boise's citizens.

Educationally, Boiseans are among the best off in the state. The Boise School District pays its teachers well for Idaho, and its students consistently score well on national tests. Boise State University has become the state's largest, and it continually strives—as it grows—to serve a growing, diverse, urban population.

Ethnically, Boise has a Euro-American majority, and the city continues its tradition of racial tolerance. There are no ghettos. Immigrants from inside and outside the U.S. settle throughout the city. A recent influx of Asian immigrants has produced no identifiable neighborhood. Whatever "cultural diversity" tendencies exist in other U.S. communities, Boise still matches the old U.S. analogy—it's a melting pot.

What does that all say? It says that Boise is O.K. What does it *mean*? That takes more study. Someone once wrote, "Anthropology is the study of *them* and sociology is the study of *us*." In Boise, as elsewhere, studying "us" is tough stuff. Really getting to know Boise's "us" requires examining Boise's culture.

Culture is the sum of society's efforts to keep life meaningful, enjoyable, and shared. Culture is truly what separates humankind from the beasts, and differences in culture most clearly differentiate human groups, whether they are families, tribes, or cities.

The significant cultural attributes of Boise appear to be religion, education, philan-

thropy, art, athletics, and an adoration of nature. The adoration of nature is discussed earlier in this book. But the other cultural attributes deserve some special attention.

...Boise still matches the old U.S. analogy— it's a melting pot.

Boise got religion as soon as it got people. The little white church on the BSU campus near the Broadway Avenue bridge is one of the oldest structures in Boise. And the Beth Israel synagogue on West State Street is said to be the oldest continuously-used Jewish temple in the U.S. west of the Mississippi River.

Jews have always been influential members of Boise society. Moses Alexander, who founded the famous Alexander's men's stores (now Alexander Davis), ran for mayor in 1897. He beat two former mayors, by two-to-one. Alexander went on to become the nation's first Jewish state governor. Boise Jews have continued to serve the city, with wholehearted involvement and generosity.

As historian Arthur Hart has often remarked, Boise possesses "a tradition of tolerance." One exception, early on, was an anti-Mormon league, organized to thwart the Latter Day Saints. Boise's Mormon community is now large and thriving. They too have provided the city with a mayor, and the LDS Church recently constructed a temple on South Cole Road.

Many Boiseans are churchgoers, as is evident on Sundays. But the city is not prudish, as is evident on Saturday nights. While not everyone dancing a Saturday night jig will warm a pew the next morning, there must be some crossovers between high spirits and the Spirit. And there is obviously a lot of crosstraining in Boise when it comes to the performing arts. There seems to be more art going on in town than the population can support.

People inner-tubing the Boise River on a hot summer evening might float by a play at the open-air Idaho Shakespeare Festival, past polka music coming from the band shell in Julia Davis Park, past a Beethoven concert at the Morrison Center for the Performing Arts, and—if they float far enough—past a Boise

Hawks baseball game at Memorial Stadium. (After all, baseball *is* a performing art.).

The Morrison Center is one of the best performing arts facilities in the world. It is large, intimate, and as well tuned as a Steinway piano. In appearance, in feel, in function, and in sound, the Morrison Center *harmonizes* its audiences with its artistic events.

The Morrison Center demonstrates the phenomenal philanthropy rampant in Boise. No city on earth deserves the generosity with which Boise's wealthier citizens have endowed their chosen home. For example, years ago Velma Morrison wanted to build for her city a performing arts center. That sounds generous enough, but Boise voters declined her gift, because the maintenance of such a wonder might cost too much. So, Mrs. Morrison came back with an operations endowment, to which Boiseans more graciously responded.

Boise's magnificent necklace of three gorgeous river parks—Julia Davis, Ann Morrison and Kathryn Albertson—are all gifts by Boise families to the city. Other gifts by individuals, groups, and corporations include the

MK Nature Center; the Discovery Center; BSU's library, pavilion, stadium, and technology center; and the future Warm Springs Avenue home for the BSU president. At times there seems to be a competition in giving.

An example of a wonderful, yet typical, gift to Boise is the Esther Simplot Performing Arts academy, built in 1992. Margie K. Stoy, Director of the Boise Philharmonic Orchestra, said, "The Simplot Academy is unique in that three major performance companies share administrative and rehearsal space, and cooperate and share resources." And they share them in a beautiful building.

The Phil, the Boise Opera, and Ballet Idaho share patrons and audiences, too. Stoy said such tremendous support for the arts is unusual, in times when Oakland, New Orleans, Sacramento, Denver and other cities are losing performing arts companies because of lack of support.

Of course, art is education. Stoy said, "One of the most exciting things for us is that the Simplot Academy has opened up a new era for the youngsters in this area, in terms of education available."

Education has a long history of cultivation in Boise. A school was established the winter after the city was organized, in 1863, 17 years before Idaho became a state. This "charter school" precedent allows an independent taxing authority and saves Boise from having to call frequent budget "override" elections whenever the Idaho State Legislature inadequately funds education. Boise is thus able to invest more dollars per student than most other school districts in Idaho (which spends less per student than nearly every other state in the union).

Boise is primarily a "public school" city. The student population recently reached 25,000, and Boise now has three senior high schools, seven junior high schools, and 32 elementary schools. Educational quality scores consistently well, and most parents don't consider sending their children to private schools. Still, private schooling is available. The Catholic schools, in particular, have long provided students with superior educations.

So far, Boise has avoided many school problems that plague other cities. Because of its comparatively homogenous demographics, Boise has not needed to bus students between neighborhoods to achieve racial integration, as have other cities such as Seattle. Violent youth gangs do not exist. Also, the high quality of the public schools has probably prevented debilitating competition from private schools. This is remarkable in light of Boise's large population of well-paid corporate executives, who one might assume would favor private schooling.

Further, both the Boise School District and the City of Boise promote the idea of neighborhood schools, in or-

There seems to be more art going on in town than the population can support.

der to strengthen the sense of community and to maintain equality of educational opportunities for students. Again, "Neighborhoods, not subdivisions," is the operating slogan. Mayor Brent Coles said that every Boise neighborhood needs "its school, its park, and its sense of a center."

Right: Cycling along the Greenbelt.
Below: BSU Pavilion.

Bronco Stadium's famous "blue turf."

A Tale of Two Cultures

The Chinese, regrettably, do not have the presence they once had in Boise. The Basques, most fortunately, continue to contribute their warmth, talent, and individuality to the city.

America, land of immigrants, has often been called "the melting pot" of cultures, when it could be more accurately termed "the grab bag." Some immigrant groups retain their ethnicities for generations, and many cities boast of their "Chinatowns" and "Little Havanas." But Boise was rarely a destination for emigrating groups, and it now presents a relatively homogenous population: white, English-speaking, and middle class. However, Boise has had its ethnic distinctions, and it retains at least one today.

Early on, Boise attracted a wide range of individual immigrants, mainly from western Europe. Scandinavian, Spanish, French and German, as well as British and Irish-English could all be heard on the city's streets. Over the years, these groups blended in with the prevailing Anglo-American society. Other ethnic groups that came a little later—for example, the Greeks and Italians—still maintain active associations.

But two distinct groups—the Chinese and the Basques—have made special contributions to Boise history and culture. The Chinese, re-grettably, do not have the presence they once had in Boise. The Basques, most fortunately, continue to contribute their warmth, talent, and individuality to the city.

Boise's China chapter began after 1869 when the transcontinental railroad was completed and Chinese laborers began to settle in Idaho. They reworked gold mines abandoned by whites, and provided white society with vegetables grown in their gardens. Garden City—the independent town nearly surrounded by Boise proper—got its name from these gardens. Garden City's main thoroughfare, Chinden Boulevard, got its name from the contraction of *CHIN*ese gar*DEN*.

By 1902, Boise's Chinese had constructed a temple. They staged banquets and parades, and held a position of respect in Boise higher than in other western cities, although the *Idaho Statesman* newspaper sometimes had to defend the Chinese when they fell victim to harassment by Boise toughs.

But by and by, Boise lost most of its Chinese population to large coastal cities such as Seattle and San Francisco.

And during the 1970s, much of Boise's "Chinatown," south of Main Street, was scraped away by bulldozers. Much of what remains of Boise Chinese culture is on exhibit at the Historical Museum.

Boise's other distinctive ethnic group is the Basques, who have helped build Boise since its first days, when Jesus Urquides ran pack trains into the mining country. Today, Boise is the center of the largest Basque community outside of Europe, and Basques distinguish themselves in all the professions.

Basque culture and language present a marvel and a mystery. The Basques have lived in the same region of Spain and France for thousands of years. They have survived and now flourish in spite of invasions and persecutions by Romans, Visigoths, Moors and others. Although most are now Roman Catholic, the Basques were not Christianized until the 10th century, and the ancient traditions survive in their folklore and in the shapes of gravestones and cultural designs.

More significantly, the Basque language exists as one of the few cultural items in the world that can be called truly unique, meaning that it is a *one-and-only*. Basque language is unrelated to any other on earth. Its roots are so ancient that a word for *knife* translates literally to "the stone that cuts." Indeed, the Basque people could be called the Original Europeans.

In Boise, they now form a community that is both close-knit and open. Perhaps this quality can be traced to the fact that most Boise Basques came from a very small region within the Basque Country. Whereas other immigrants may have come to American cities and sought like-speaking strangers with whom to fashion new "little old-countries," the Basques who came to Boise were already bonded. Their ethnicity secure, Boise Basques have been able to mix and even intermarry without losing their cultural identity.

Boise State University scholar Dr. Pat Beiter recalled that when he first visited the Basque country in 1974, he had been asked by a Boise sheepherder, who was nicknamed Moixo, to take a present to Moixo's sister. "But," Beiter said, "when we drove to Moixo's town, I realized that—my God!—I didn't know Moixo's real name." And Moixo had been in Boise for 34 years.

It didn't matter. At the first door they came to, a woman asked, "Are you Pat?"

Early on, many Boise Basques lived around Grove and River streets. This community was so "tight" that many children learned no English until they started school. Now Boise's Basque children learn English first, but there is strong support for Basque culture, including a Basque Studies program at Boise State University and a 20-year tradition of BSU students—both Basques and non-Basques—studying in the old country.

Basque culture can be enjoyed at the Oñati Restaurant on Chinden Boulevard, and at the Basque Center and Museum and the Bar Gernika, along Boise's "Basque Row" on Grove Street. In front of the museum, there stands an oak that grew from a shoot taken from the famous Tree of Gernika, a symbol of Basque tradition.

Left: Basque dancers at Jaialdi festival, Old Idaho Pen.
Below: Ancient Basque culture at St. John's Cathedral.

88

Disappearing tradition—Basque sheepherder and his helpers.

Slightly more than one half of Boise public school students go on to college immediately after graduating. This reflects a national trend. Nontraditional students—those over the age of 25—now make up one half of the students at

---

Students can learn outside of the classroom, in exciting settings offering practical experiences...

Boise State University.

BSU strives to fulfill their needs, as it serves the interests of the city. A good university is so crucial to a city that former BSU President John Keiser is fond of saying, "There has never been a great city without a great university."

This is more than a paraphrase of that old cowboy joke, "If we had some ham we could make ham sandwiches, *if* we had some bread." Boise and BSU go together like ham on rye, and the greatness of one depends on the excellence of the other.

Advertising itself as an *urban* university, BSU offers its students an education unavailable elsewhere in Idaho. Students can learn outside of the classroom, in exciting settings offering practical experiences: medical training in two large hospitals; governmental insights at the state legislature; journalism internships at the state's largest newspaper; and employment opportunities at national and multinational corporations.

BSU's primary emphases are business and economics, social sciences, public affairs, performing arts, and interdisciplinary studies. Through its seven colleges and two schools, the university offers 120 major fields of interest, 57 baccalaureate degree programs, 20 vocational technical degrees, and 21 graduate and 21 associate degree programs. With an operating budget of $100 million, BSU supports a faculty of nearly 580, and most classes are taught by full-time professors, not by graduate assistants.

This range of course opportunities is matched by the range of students. Many of BSU's 15,000 students may come fresh from Idaho's high schools, but many come from other states and foreign countries. This results partly from the fact that BSU is an educa-

tional bargain, and partly from the growing reputation of BSU, Boise, and Idaho.

More noticeable, perhaps, is the presence of the nontraditional students. These include mothers who have raised and educated their children; retired persons who want to enrich their lives; and people who have spent time out in the real world of business and the military, and who want to switch careers or enhance their employability. Many BSU students "have been there," to use a colloquial phrase. And the younger students benefit from their seasoned perspectives *and* from their academic competition. Professors like it, too. Education professor Pat Beiter said, "BSU is the best teaching assignment you could ask for." Of course, he said this as he stared from his office window at a fine trout stream 50 yards away.

BSU's 110-acre campus sits right on the Boise River, offering students access to the extensive Greenbelt paths system and easy walking distances to downtown, the Park Center corporate village, and loads of culture and entertainment, including the Idaho Shakespeare Festival's open-air theater, The Flicks "alternative" movie house, and the string of lively restaurants and bars up and down Main Street.

BSU students share Boise with its citizens, and Boiseans share in BSU activities. On-campus facilities include the Morrison Center for the Performing Arts, with its finely tuned 2,000-seat hall; Bronco Stadium, with its eye-catching "Bronco blue" turf; and the 12,000-seat Pavilion, which has hosted rodeos, NCAA basketball tournaments, and The Grateful Dead rock group. BSU fields exciting teams in many sports. Football, basketball and wrestling have long been favorites in Boise, and lately gymnastics, tennis, and women's basketball have caught fire.

One great example of how the University serves its community is the BSU Radio network. Publisher and poet Alan Minskoff said that BSU Radio is "the best thing that's happened to Boise." In 1985, KBSU was affectionately referred to as "the voice of the riverbank" and "the wind in the willows," because of its feeble signal. Now, thanks to the leadership of the station manager, Dr. Jim Paluzzi, 600,000 people can pick up one or more of BSU's radio services. Among

those are: KBSX, with local and world news, including the BBC; KBSM-FM, with arts and performances; and KBSM-AM, with "multi-cultural service," including "World Cafe" and "National Native News." BSU Radio staff have jeeped and hiked their power-boosting equipment to the tops of so many mountains that now southern Idaho, with its isolated valleys, has the best public radio service in the nation.

Boise is so nuts about sports that Boise Parks and Recreation, the YMCA, the Boise School District, BSU, and other organizations can barely keep up with demand. From spring through fall, Boise parks swarm. In winter, Bogus Basin offers tremendous day and night skiing. KTVB-TV Sports Director Larry Maneely said Boise's involvement in sports compares with that of Sacramento, a much bigger city.

For softball, volleyball, flag football, and basketball, the Boise Parks and Recreation Department sponsors 24,000 players on 1,300 teams. That doesn't count the wildly popular organized soccer league games and countless "pick-up" contests. Willow Lane and the new 160-acre Simplot Sports Complex help provide

adequate space, but Boiseans say they want and need more.

Boise State University will probably move its football program from the Big Sky Conference to the bigger Big West. An average 4,000 fans attend Boise Hawks home baseball games. For 1992, 2,300 season tickets were sold, second only to Buffalo, New York, for minor league teams. Boise even fields a

---

...BSU Radio is "the best thing that's happened to Boise."

---

hockey team, the Boise Blades, although they must practice on frozen ponds.

Larry Maneely said one interesting thing about Boise is that "organized sports have really gotten organized." He compared today's youth sports to those of his own youth, when little league really meant "little." Nowadays, Boise kids will belong to several teams in several sports, with great coaching and parental support. Boise youth teams, in sports such as soccer, compete on a national level.

Corporate Village

When Greg Eby was growing up on Boise's west bench, most of his playmates were the sons of small businessmen. When he and his family recently moved to Pier Pointe, he was surprised that his neighbors all seemed to work for big corporations. Boise was never a "company town," but it has become a corporate village.

Several major corporations are headquartered in Boise. They employ thousands of people, and they concentrate a large cadre of executives in the city. This partly explains the high percentage of upscale homes and the rapid development of expensive view lots. It also explains much of the character of the city. Boise corporations encourage their employees to take active parts in community affairs.

The large corporations recruit many of their executives from outside the area, but Boise natives fit right in. John Keiser recalled teaching one of his first history classes at BSU: "We discussed the Panic of 1837, which was the nation's first depression. It really hit the eastern cities hard, and its effects included the first real trade union movement and experiments with utopian socialism.

"I asked my students what they would have done then, if they were out of work and hungry. To my surprise, they said they'd look for a business opportunity, work hard, and maybe even expand through a sale of stock.

"This," Keiser said, "is the entrepreneurial spirit with a vengeance."

It surprised him then, but it also may have inspired him. He went on to become a dynamic president of BSU, a candidate for mayor of Boise, and most recently president of Southwest Missouri State University.

John Keiser is one example of many Boise success stories. But get-ahead gumption can't explain all the big business. And a glance at the map suggests Boise would do better as a local distribution center than as a world headquarters. True, Boise has ready access to transportation, with a rail line, an interstate highway, and a full-service airport, but it is far from large markets or other centers of commerce. Geographically, the best one could say about Boise is that

Every Boise visitor asks, "Whose is that?" That home on the hill belongs to J.R. and Esther Simplot.

it is equally far from everyplace else.

Why Boise, then, for so much big business? Each company has its special reasons, but shared explanations exist. A few companies are here because they started here. Most are here because their employees like it here. And many are here because of the much-mentioned work ethic, which prevails among potential employees.

Almost as famous as Idaho's "famous potatoes" is Boise entrepreneur J.R. Simplot, who heads the J.R. Simplot Company, which has nearly 400 Boise employees, and almost 9,000 total in North America.

Many have called Jack Simplot "the Potato King," but he is also a kind of Renaissance man. In this day of specialists, Simplot is both visionary and generalist, an entrepreneur with a long view to the future and a practiced eye for opportunity. His bold savvy, rough graciousness, and generosity are legendary.

In 1923, at age 14, Simplot left school to work at odd jobs and earn enough money to buy some livestock. Seventy years later, his still privately-held company has annual revenues of $1.6 billion. Simplot said, "One of the smartest things I've ever done is hire good, honest, hardworking people, and turn them loose." But it is obvious that he turns

Geographically, the best one could say about Boise is that it is equally far from everyplace else.

them loose in profitable directions.

It is just as obvious that J.R. Simplot sees well in all directions, because one of the traits he is most famous for is the ability to work all of the angles of any enterprise. "Use it all," could be a Simplot slogan, whether that means agricultural products or an employee's brains, imagination, and gumption. His company has grown and processed vegetables, and then used all the by-products—for animal feed, fertilizer, energy production, and even as habitat for a species of Egyptian warm-water fish that is sold as a culinary delicacy.

The Morrison Knudsen Corporation got its start in 1912 when Harry Morrison approached M.H. Knudsen about going into business with him. "How much money have you got?" Knudsen asked him. "No money," Morrison said, "just guts."

MK is now a part of American history and big player in America's future. MK's heavy construction projects have included the Hoover and Grand Coulee dams. Under the direction of Boise native Bill Agee, is now a manufacturing, engineering, construction and environmental services company with 1,300 Boise employees, 13,500 worldwide, and 1992 revenues of $2 billion. MK is major contractor in visionary projects, such as a high-speed rail system in Texas and the Super Conducting-Super Collider subnuclear research facility.

Like Boise's other corporations, MK and its employees devote many hours to Boise's betterment. But two recent MK projects deserve special attention. One is the creation of the MK Idaho Department of Fish and Game Nature

Center, one of the finest stream aquariums in the nation. The other is the restoration of the historic Boise railway depot, the handsomest landmark in Boise. These two contributions to education and history are absolutely priceless.

Another Boise business that began with "a man and a plan" is Albertson's, Inc., which probably touches more Americans every day than Boise's other big corporations combined. Joe Albertson opened his first grocery store in Boise, at the corner of 16th and State streets in 1939. In 1992, Albertson's opened 107 new stores, and annual sales surpassed $10 billion. By the end of 1993, it intends to be operating 656 stores in 19 states, employing over 2,600 people in Ada County, and 71,000 nationwide. It is the sixth-largest retail food-drug chain in the U.S.

Albertson's has a commercial slogan that goes, "It's your store." It is certainly Boise's. The Albertson's company, its employees, and the founding Albertson family have contributed immensely to Boise's quality of life. A walk through Kathryn Albert-son Park or an afternoon at the BSU library give only a fragmentary indication. Albertson's list of contributions to Boise must be an "Idaho mile" long.

West One Bancorp goes back to 1867, when C.W. Moore opened his bank in the back of a store only a stone's throw from the present headquarters. By 1993, it had grown to a $7.4 billion company with 4,500 employees in four states.

West One contributes financial and volunteer support to many community organizations. Chairman Dan Nelson served as founding chairman of the Boise River Festival, helping to ensure the event's success. And *that's* just the boss. West One's Stuart Johnson said that company employees probably take part in every event in the city.

Longtime Boise resident Boise Cascade Corporation began life as the Boise Payette Lumber Company on Christmas Eve 1913 when it purchased the Barber Lumber Company on the Boise River, just upstream from town. It now has about 850 Boise employees and over 17,000 workers in the U.S. and Canada. It manufactures and distributes paper and paper products, office products, and building products. To support these operations, Boise Cascade owns and manages tree farms in Idaho and elsewhere, and it harvests timber on National Forest lands. With annual sales of about $3.7 billion, Boise Cascade ranks 134th on *Fortune* magazine's list of the 500 largest U.S. manufacturing companies.

Like Boise's other corporations, MK and its employees devote many hours to Boise's betterment.

Chairman of the Board and CEO John Fery said, "Boise's appealing lifestyle, with its excellent mix of recreational opportunities and cultural activities, is an incentive for retaining good employees." Fery likes the way "city, county, and state government, as well as education, work with and support local companies." He said Boiseans generally "view business as making a contri-

City Hall fountain and West One Bank, on The Grove.

Right: *The old fire house.*
Below: *The Simplot Sports Complex at Columbia Village.*

bution to the success of the area," contrary to the anti-business sentiment found in some other communities.

Boise Cascade has long contributed to civic projects in Boise, including donating land for parks and educational buildings, providing and planting 100 trees down Capitol Boulevard; sponsoring opera, ballet, and philharmonic performances; holding a literacy rally and donating books to elementary schools; and proudly fostering a special partnership with Boise High School. During tough times in the forest products industry, Boise Cascade volunteers have met the need that monetary contributions once met. Boise Cascade people worked in 33 volunteer projects during 1992, with over 300 individuals participating.

TJ International began operations in Boise in 1960, when Art Troutner teamed his technological genius with the organizational skills of Harold Thomas to begin producing "engineered" wood products, revolutionizing the construction industry.

TJI's substitutes for old-growth forest lumber provide ecologically friendlier meth-ods of construction. Wal-Mart used TJI products to build its prototype "ecostore," conserving the equivalent of 87 trees that are 18 inches in diameter and 120 feet tall. Both technologically and philosophically, TJI promotes nature conservation.

In 1992, TJI rebounded from the deepest housing recession since World War II and set an all-time sales record of $400 million, a 41 percent increase over 1991. TJI employs 3,400 people, 123

> ### *"You just don't grow up in our neck of the woods thinking someone can outwork you."*

in Boise. Many of TJI's "owner investors" live in Boise, and they contribute greatly to its quality of life.

Ore-Ida Foods is one of the largest processors of frozen foods in the United States and the leading retail brand of frozen potato products. Ore-Ida moved operations to Boise in 1968, mainly for geographic reasons; Boise was in between its two factories in Ontario and Burley. Out of a company total of more than 4,000 employees, Ore-Ida's Boise employees now number about 400 at corporate headquarters in ParkCenter, along the Boise Greenbelt.

Ore-Ida's employees enjoy what they call, "an unbeatable quality of life." Ilene Harsip is an associate manager at Ore-Ida and a recent transplant from Boston. She said she also likes "the mix of the other transplants," adding, "I find my neighbors and coworkers are from everywhere," and share "an interest in and commitment to the community."

Ore-Ida and its employees support many cultural and athletic events. For nine years, the company was the anchor sponsor of the Ore-Ida Woman's Challenge, the nation's premier cycling event for women. It sponsors the Tater Tots Tennis Tournament for area youth, helping establish Boise as one of the top tennis towns in the country.

Ore-Ida's many beneficiaries include the Boise Opera and the Boise Philharmonic Orchestra, Ballet Idaho, and the Idaho Shakespeare Festival, whose shoreline theater shares Ore-Ida's ParkCenter corporate campus.

Micron Technology, Inc., knows what it's doing in Boise. It's manufacturing high-quality semiconductor components by using high-quality employees. According to Micron Vice President Kipp Bedard, "Our team members are hardworking and motivated to succeed." The challenge to American microchip manufacturers is seen as an incentive at Micron. CEO Joe Parkinson once told a *Forbes* magazine reporter, "You just don't grow up in our neck of the woods thinking someone can outwork you."

A good example of Micron's manufacturing expertise is its 466 Magnum personal computer, which won *PC Magazine's* "Editor's Choice" award for 1993. Still another example is Micron's decision to concentrate itself in Boise. Bedard said, "The integration of research, manufacturing and support function in Boise enables us to achieve high quality, decreased production times, and increased yields." And all of this while Micron employees donate many hours to their community.

Education receives much of Micron's attention. The company has donated over $6.5 million to education since 1984, and Joe Parkinson serves on the state board of education. Upper-level managers sit on the boards of

Hewlett-Packard is one of the first large electronics manufacturers to end completely its use of ozone-damaging chlorofluorocarbons.

many community organizations, and many employees participate in activities such as the Partners in Education Program.

Micron employs 4,700 in Boise, with a payroll of over $150 million. In fiscal 1993, net sales increased 19 percent to over $700 million.

Unlike Micron, the Hewlett-Packard Company did not begin with a bang in Boise. It started in a small garage in the San Francisco Bay area and now manufactures

some of the world's best electronic products, including the finest laser printers and data disk drives. Since it began its Boise operations in 1973, HP has grown to one of Idaho's largest employers, with 5,000 full-time Boise employees.

Like Micron, Hewlett-Packard and its employees are full partners in every aspect of Boise life. A good example is HP's concern for the environment. Hewlett-Packard is one of the first large electronics manufacturers to end completely its use of ozone-damaging chlorofluorocarbons. HP is also teaming up with the City of Boise and the YMCA to build a major West Boise public sports complex.

If Boise serves as a hometown for big business, then one might assume that emergent area ventures have the potential to go big time. And several Boise-area enterprises appear to be on the edge of greatness.

Phil Reed had already made his reputation with his development of the Computerland and Businessland chains. But his love of flying made him want to do more—to give America *what it really needs:* a fun, affordable airplane.

Above: *Roasted daily—White Cloud Mountain Coffee.*
Left: *SkyStar's Kit Fox.*

Facing page: *Idaho State Capitol.*

Reed also loved the Boise area, and in 1992 he moved to Boise and purchased Dan Denny's highly admired kit airplane business, at the Nampa Airport. Phil Reed said the Boise area is a great place for his business. He is "always impressed by the honesty and character and work ethic here." Many potential customers who visit his Nampa research and production facility stay several days to enjoy the Boise area. Several "liked it so much they moved here."

Reed is now using his personal vision and his business acumen to bring his dreams to reality. SkyStar Aircraft's new two-seater, the *Vixen*, weighs only 500 pounds, but it carries 700 pounds of people, fuel and cargo, at a maximum speed of 133 m.p.h. and a range of 700 miles. Its power-on stall speed is a only 28 m.p.h., which compares favorably with a feather.

Some aviation experts have wagered that the *Vixen* will be the first small American airplane to be FAA-certified for factory production since the glory days of Cessna and Piper.

That would be fine with Phil Reed. But he said SkyStar itself will probably stick with producing high quality, affordable kit aircraft. "With a kit plane, the customer develops a real passion. And working with this kind of customer keeps our passions high and makes this business a great one." Reed has entertained the possibility of going into a joint venture with a company better acquainted with factory-style sales and service.

SkyStar's status as aviation pioneer fits in well with Boise's history. Boise was one of the first cities to get com-

> *"There's not a river person anywhere who hasn't heard about Idaho."*

mercial air passenger service, with United Airlines' parent company Varney Air, in 1926.

While the *Vixen* may seem to defy gravity, another local enterprise uses gravity to make a profit. The Maravia Corporation, headquartered in Garden City, builds and markets inflatable boats—rafts, kayaks, cata-rafts, and rigid inflatables—test-driven on the famous whitewater near Boise.

In 1985, two Idaho river outfitters—Mike McLeod and Doug Tims—heard that Maravia, then located in California, was up for sale. "We liked Maravia's boats," said McLeod, "And so we bought the company. But no way was I going to move to Marin County." and so with the help of the California plant manager and all-new Boise employees, they relaunched Maravia in Idaho. Gross sales volume is now increasing at 30 percent a year.

McLeod said Idaho offers Maravia a great mix of fine employees, good life style, and a natural laboratory for the research and development of their products. "The Payette system is fantastic. "I don't know of another river system like it." The Payette offers up to Class V whitewater, within an hour of Boise. And Idaho offers Maravia a perfect product tie-in. McLeod said, "There's not a river person anywhere who hasn't heard about Idaho."

Garden City also serves as headquarters and roasting center for the up-and-running success of the White Cloud

Mountain Coffee Company, parent of the Moxie Java coffeehouse chain. Jerome Eberharter and his friends have taken what once was a big-city phenomenon and shown that it can work well in Boise. Indeed, it has worked so well in Boise that Moxie Java has expanded into the "caffeine capital" of Seattle. Moxie now has 14 coffeehouses, in Idaho, Oregon, Washington and Arizona. Eberharter's goal is 500 coffee "carts, kiosks and cafes."

Moxie spokeswoman Annie Hesp admitted, "Boise is in the middle of nowhere, but it works great for us. Jerome's idea is to have happy employees, and here we get a great lifestyle."

Finally, Boise's economy doesn't run on pure capitalism. While many Boise businesses flourish in spite of Boise's isolation, government in Boise has prospered because of it. Being "equally far" from other large cities has fostered Boise's growth as a governmental center. And serving as a center for legislation and bureaucracy moderates Boise's financial swings in times of economic transition.

Boise serves as Idaho's state capital, which ensures its position as the headquarters of most state agencies and brings in lawmakers every year to spend everybody's money. Boise is also a federal center of some size, providing an effective administrative location for the U.S. Courts, Boise National Forest, Bureau of Land Management, Veterans Administration, Bureau of Reclamation, Fish and Wildlife Service, National Interagency Fire Center, and the Army and Air National Guards.

The expected "peace dividend" from the end of the Cold War has turned out to be a big one for Boise. Ironically, Boise has increased its military muscle. The Army and Air Guards have both been expanded, Gowen Field is growing, and nearby Mountain Home Air Force Base now serves as a "composite wing" air base, ensuring its position as one Idaho's biggest employers. Not since the original Boise Barracks and then World War II has the military meant so much to the Boise economy.

"Boise is in the middle of nowhere, but it works great for us. Jerome's idea is to have happy employees, and here we get a great lifestyle."

Fishing the Boise.

Right: Sun Valley residents.
Below: Shirley Riebe at Edwards' Nursery.

A Nostalgia for Now

A human-sized humanity helps many Boiseans feel at home. Boiseans are immediately friendly (this bothers some big city folk) and at present there's no wrong side of town.

How does one best paint a picture of a city? Any single piece of information provides a fragmentary point of view.

The Present is fleeting; it lasts as long as a breath. Although photographs and "facts" give a snapshot of a moment, they exclude the looming, sometimes dooming, peripheries.

The Past—history—is always changing; it changes with the needs and beliefs of the Present. Depending on one's own bias, Boise's past can be seen as a great testament to the human spirit or as just another example of "westering" exploitation.

The Future is anyone's story to tell. It's an expectant fiction, residing in the public domains of hope, optimism, anxiety, and gloom. Pick any individual human emotion and there you will find someone's private vision of the future.

But visions of the future often serve one great purpose. They illuminate the concerns of the present. Boiseans' visions of the future reveal much about the city.

For one thing, many Boiseans feel nostalgic for *now*. There is a sense in the city that "this is as good as it gets." That's compared to the past, compared to the future, and compared to nearly every other city in America. "This is the future that we should all work for" is how many Boiseans feel about Boise *today*.

Nearness to nature is a major reason many Boiseans love Boise. Nature crosses the city's heart with the Greenbelt, and embraces it with millions of acres of forest and high desert wilderness.

A human-sized humanity helps many Boiseans feel at home. Boiseans are immediately friendly (this bothers some big city folk) and at present there's no wrong side of town. And, "You're never anonymous in Boise," said urban historian Todd Shallat. "Wherever you go, whatever you do, there is somebody there who knows you." This fosters a sense of personal responsibility, which perhaps contributes to Boise's low rate of crime.

Access to culture endears Boise to many. As the cultural center for 300 miles around and the "favorite niece" of many citizen-benefactors, Boise offers symphony, ballet, drama and other fine arts at a per-capita rate that is seldom excelled. And the folk-ier arts of rock, blues, film, and comedy are a growing Boise treasure. As Peter Johnson said, "Boise already offers much more than you can hope to take in."

Boise advertises itself—and exposes itself—as *the place* to live the good life. This book is one example. And every new month seems to bring out more magazine and newspaper stories, extolling the city's virtues. *Business Week*, *Money*, and *Pacific Northwest* magazines have raved about the city. An *Outside* magazine cover photo of Boise's Hyde Park was even featured on the back of a box of Kellogg's cereal. The *Outside* article asked its readers, "Why aren't you living here?"

Some Boiseans might think that the answer is, "Because you can't sell your house in L.A." According to Todd Shallat, many newcomers see Boise as "the city of their own lost youths," whether that city was Denver, Minneapolis, or San Jose. They come here to claim something that may never have been, but that *should have been*. Boise feels like family, fishing, ball games, and fun.

Many a newcomer thinks the city got too big, "the day after I moved in." In-migration puts enormous pressure on Boise, increasing congestion, pollution, traffic and crime.

More established residents agree. East-ender Amy Stahl said, "Boise is under siege." She loves her little house in her older neighborhood. She loves the nearly instant gratification Boise now provides for her needs for Nature. But she pointed to the rapidly rising tower of St. Luke's Hospital and wonders how many more little houses and quiet streets will fall victim to Boise's growth.

Always now, there are questions of limits. Will Boiseans want to wall out newcomers to keep Boise as it is? Will wildlands managers have to fence off Nature— from Boiseans—to protect it from getting loved to death? Limits seem anathema to the Western tradition. Robert Frost wrote, "Something there is that does not love a wall." And Westerners have long fought barbed wire and governmental regulation. If they don't win the fight, they move farther west.

But nowadays Boise—and the Mountain States—is as far West as you can get. In many ways, this is the end of the line of a poetic, barbaric, magnificent story.

Some people say, "Stop it all now. Fence it and save it." But Pug Ostling and others ask, "Do we build fences or gates?" Gates, they imply, guarantee us access, neighborliness, and responsibility. Don't fence it; finesse it. Find a way. This goes both for the pristine wilderness and for booming Boise. Opportunities abound.

Many a newcomer thinks the city got too big, "the day after I moved in."

Right now, many Boiseans feel like they have it all: a shared community, which encourages belonging; personal privacy, which allows a sense of dignity; and access to Nature, which guarantees renewal. Boise is not the best of all possible worlds. But in this era of limits, it may be as good as it gets.

Below: *Another look.*

Facing page, top: *Boise's "Bird Man," Morlan Nelson, with a peregrine falcon (and a wathchful dog).*
Bottom: *Relaxing by Park Center Pond.*

Index

Clay Morgan grew up in Boise. He now lives in McCall with his wife Barbara and their two sons. He has written for newspapers, magazines, and radio. His novel *Santiago and the Drinking Party* (Viking/Penguin) won a 1992 Pacific Northwest Booksellers Award.

Steve Bly is known in the region as a photographer, travel professional, and outdoor activist. He lives on the banks of the Boise River with his wife Pam. His work has been published regionally and nationally, in such publications as *Sunset, Pacific Northwest,* and *Outsider* magazines. He is represented by AllStock and F. Stock photo agencies.

Boise's backyard—Centennial Marsh on Camas Prairie.